Stop, Look, Choose

Your Journey to Peace and Freedom

By Joni Lerner, B.Msc.

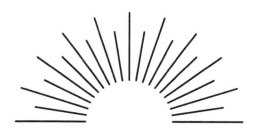

STOP, LOOK, CHOOSE

Cover art by Joni Lerner, M.Bsc.

Your life is like a textured stone.
Time to polish it.

To John

Thank you for being my companion, partner, guide and love. Standing by your side and seeing the Universe through your playful yet wise lens has opened up infinite possibilities. Our match has set me free in profound and unexpected ways. I thank you for your loving influence. It will be paid forward in this book.

Foreword
By Allie Michelle

When I was thirteen years old, my mother and I lay on the floor of my bedroom with crystals on our foreheads. Those who don't believe in magic will never notice when it is right in front of their nose, and my mother always taught me to see through eyes of wonder. Dad was traveling to the middle east three weeks out of the month, and so the two of us had our own Gilmore Girls season of lighting the spark in one another. Practicality was tossed out the window. We danced in our socks, sang loud enough to rattle glass, made burritos, and went to crystal shops. We painted in the backyard, spoke about our dreams as though they had already happened, and read books thick enough to double as a weapon. We took sick days off school and went camping in the forest, as she taught me how to paint and appreciate the simple beauty of being alive.

Most people spend decades gleaning degrees, or travel across the world to acquire glittering certifications. There is value in this, yes. However, I cannot imagine a job that prepares someone more to acquire wisdom than motherhood. Arguably the most important task in the world is raising another human being, and my mom excelled in flying colors. Her wisdom was not earned in a fluorescent lit classroom, but in the trenches of motherhood. Decades of devotion to another human being prepared her to speak on trusting life, letting go of control, and finding her spark again after years of selflessness. She raised me to turn my pain into art, follow the beating compass in my chest, and shut out everyone else's opinions as I paved my own path.

I always knew there was a well of wisdom within her, waiting to spill onto the world. After having the privilege of editing and producing this book with her, I now see it. A tidal wave of love, compassion, and snappy humor sweeps these pages. She manages to take profound wisdom that is often indigestible and weave it into her own life story, creating a level of relatability that demystifies the spiritual path.

I am of course biased in my opinions of this book, given that she is my hero for her courage and guidance over the years. However, as a best-selling author and veracious reader I will say: this book is a timeless piece of art that anyone can find a piece of themselves in. It is raw, profound, and gloriously human. I will return to it again and again and look forward to passing it down to my own children someday.

With love,
Allie Michelle
3x best-selling author and spoken word artist

Introduction

Welcome!

Have you ever thought there must be more to life? Have you ever wondered if there is a next level to your life or wondered what that next level is? If you have, then you have come to one of those important choice points in life by opening this book.

Truth be told, you are here, right now wherever you are in life, because you are ready to go to the next level. I can say this with certainty, because this is the way Life has set up all Life, of which you are a unique part.

You can coach yourself on a path to peace, joy, abundance, and self-acceptance. To open your heart and your mind to all possibilities.

This book will guide you through thought-provoking statements to open your mind. Those statements are pulled from my social media posts, personal musings, and foundational themes of my coaching through the years.

You will then have an opportunity to list your three gratitudes for the day to raise your energetic vibration. Learning to consistently be in a mindset of gratitude will change your brain chemistry, release toxins, and cause good hormones to be produced. You are also given explanations and stories so that you can go deeper.

These stories are from my life experience. In them, I reveal the ups and downs of my path. Your life could be similar or very different in so many ways but that doesn't mean that you can't use my stories to open your mind and your heart. Don't compare yourself to me or to anyone. Use others (including me) to learn and grow.

Finally, the questions and affirmations at the end of each segment invite you to become aware of your conscious and unconscious beliefs, clear them, and be free. Know that if you "live" this book, there will be physiological changes in your mind and body.

The format of the chapters and the entire book is designed to facilitate two distinct methods of learning. They are:

Awaken –
defined as increasing awareness through education and discovery using personal application and reflection to integrate what you discover here.

Activate –
application of awakening to daily thinking, routines, and ways of being.

A key question you may have is, "If I read this book and do what is in this book (Awaken and Activate), what is the value I can create?" The combination of the guidance of this book and your commitment will produce the most sought-after result in history: Peace.

This is about becoming aware and curious regarding what's driving your life beneath the surface. It is designed to help you process and change those driving thoughts, beliefs, and habits for good. The daily affirmation is designed to reinforce your new learnings.

You may choose to do one entry a day for 90 days or pace yourself. There is no particular order so you can also jump around if you choose. There is no right way to do this as you will receive the benefits regardless. Absorb and process this in your own time. If resistance arises, notice it. And keep going. If emotions arise, embrace them and allow them to pass through like a wave. Even if all you do is read the daily quote, you can shift your perspective.

This is not meant to be or replace therapy. It is also not meant to be consumed all at once like a novel. Instead, it's an opportunity for self-exploration through a form of coaching. To uncover what works and does not and discover new levels of self-empowerment and abundance.

If you are reading this book and expect immediate and profound results, you may be disappointed and tempted to give up. Don't fall into this trap. Embrace the journey. Embrace your life. Embrace learning or not learning. Embracing anything includes acceptance and integration. It is the key to this book and your happiness.

Read it slowly, savor the wisdom and golden nuggets you may find and integrate the learnings into your experience. If you are ready to jump in and change your life, turn the page and begin!

One last suggestion. I encourage you to use a companion journal of your choosing where you will have all the room you need to express your thoughts, respond to the prompts, and make any notes you need to support your full expression and release. It is written and shared with all my heart.

— *Joni*

Day 1

When you make a decision to accept nothing less than emotional intimacy and whole-hearted love, you honor your true worth.

Three things for which I am grateful...

1. _____

2. _____

3. _____

You are worthy of connection, companionship, intimacy, self-acceptance, and love. You are both connected to everything, and at the same time, the center of your human experience. In fact, you are worthy simply by virtue of being born uniquely you.

Looking back, I can see all the ways that I dishonored myself by not demanding wholehearted love and emotional intimacy. I didn't know I deserved it. I also had no clue how to give it. I chose the next best thing—someone who wouldn't purposefully hurt me. I was playing not to lose because I didn't have the experience in my life of unconditional love. Rather than trust that the right man for me would appear as I matured and healed, I would settle for someone who filled the space. As if we were actors and he would fill the leading man role. I didn't realize that I was trying to fill the hole of loneliness with another person. The hole is essentially caused by not being connected to your own Divinity. The lie that we are fed, is that we need our Other Half to be worthy in this society. It's not true.

I want you to actually decide to accept (and give) nothing less than wholehearted love and emotional intimacy from here forward. You won't do it perfectly but why not make a start?

What will that look like? How will you be with others?

_____

_____

_____

_____

How will you be that for yourself?

_____

_____

_____

_____

_____

What has gotten in the way of this in the past?

_____

_____

_____

_____

Affirmation:
"Today I am whole-hearted, and I honor my worth."

Day 2

People often tell a story to themselves and others about who they think they are based on what has happened in the past. But that's just a story repeated through time. Given that you alone are the author of your story, why not make it worthy of who you truly are?

Three things for which I am grateful...

1. _____
2. _____
3. _____

We all have stories. Or do they have us?

The story I told myself was that I was too much. I came from a childhood, like many others, that was chaotic and unsafe. In my case, there was alcoholism, mental illness, financial insecurity (bill collectors were allowed to speak to children back then), infidelity, divorce, and instability. Sounds like the perfect recipe for learning how to be a happy well-adjusted human, yes? Energetically, I embodied the chaos. I rode a motorcycle, dyed my hair burgundy, wore long acrylic nails, and as for my friends, the more messed up the better because it made me feel like I wasn't the worst one in the room. The story I told was that because of my terrible, awful, no-good, stinky childhood and family of origin, I couldn't be happy, and I couldn't have healthy relationships. I certainly couldn't be successful. I later learned that I had a belief that I couldn't outshine my mother. That was the limiting belief that kept me from following my dreams for years. Was it true? No. It was a lie born from my childhood perspective that I needed to dim my light to keep the peace. I shine all over the place now. I am authentically me and if someone has a negative response to that, I know that it's their problem. Not mine. Shine. Shine. Shine.

What is the story you tell yourself?

What is the new story you will learn to live?
Write this story from the point of view of inner strength and worthiness. The story needs to be in the present tense and have you at the center. Winning. Loving. Living with courage. Now, imagine that you are already the person you dream of being in your story and write the narrative. Pay attention to how you feel in the story.

Who are the other characters? Are they supportive?

_____

_____

_____

_____

_____

_____

What are the milestones of your hero?

_____

_____

_____

_____

_____

_____

_____

You can write this story again at the end of the ninety days and
see just how powerful this journey to a better you has been.
Take up space.

Affirmation:
"I am deeply worthy."

𝔇ay 3

All around is evidence. Choose to focus on the evidence of positivity. That's what will grow.

Three things for which I am grateful...

1. _____
2. _____
3. _____

Stop looking at the negative. Instead, look at the positive in your life to manifest change. In this journey, you are rewiring your brain to seek the positive, which will bring you to new levels of peace and abundance. Since the beginning of time, your brain and its primitive limbic system are wired to survive. The caveman's very existence depended on looking for the negative and reacting to it. The snake in the tree, the woolly mammoth, fire, rival tribes. But in today's world, with tens of thousands of pieces of information assaulting you daily, it has become exhausting and overwhelming to process the input in old ways. It can be triggering. So, rewire your brain by actively looking for the positive and celebrating even the tiniest of wins. High five your friend when you have a win. If you're alone, high five yourself.

At 10 years old, my sister's nickname was Tigger. Positive, bouncy, lively, happy, joyous, and infinitely lovable. My nickname was Eeyore. Negative, sluggish, sarcastic, and always with a glass half empty. We were raised in the same household and with the same set of challenges, but her outlook was very different. It took years and years for me to realize that I was living in victim mode already. I thought life wasn't fair. We moved too much. My sister was prettier than me. Dad loved her more. My other sister made my life hell (mental illness and drug addiction). I took everything personally.

And I slimed everyone around me with my negativity and self-centeredness. If I could talk to little me, I would say lighten up baby, life is a wild ride and you get to choose how it goes. Focus on what is joyful and positive and you will receive that back tenfold, I promise you. Little me would have spit in my face but I would have let her know, "It's ok, sweetheart, it gets better." Trust and believe. The key is looking at the positive. Looking at what is working and creating more and more and more of that. I am living proof that a profound shift in perspective can change your entire life and you are not a victim of anyone or anything.

Begin looking at the positive in your life.
This can be as simple as the coffee you drink in the morning, to the hugs you give, to the view outside your window to the $ in your bank. Write it all out.

My life is abundant and joyful in the following ways...

_____

_____

_____

_____

_____

_____

_____

_____

_____

_____

Affirmation:
"I choose to see the wonder all around and live in gratitude."

𝔇ay 4

If you want a hug, give a hug. If you want to feel joy, be joyful. If you want love, give love. How you show up to the party is what you will create in your reality.

Three things for which I am grateful...

1. _____
2. _____
3. _____

Invariably, how you show up to life is what will be reflected back. The old mentality is that you want something and can't figure out why that person or the Universe is not providing it. What's true is that what you put out will come back. So, what you are and do each day will directly influence your experience.

When I rode horses with another mom and our kids back in the day, we would talk about life as we meandered through the trails. I would say how I needed an office chair for my desk, and I drove around the corner and someone had put the exact chair out on the sidewalk for trash pickup. So, I picked it up. Or how I had parking karma and always got a spot right out front no matter where I went. Or that my mother and kids had found snow saucers in the attic and we were all hysterically "dirt bombing" down the hill in the backyard. She stopped her horse and looked me in the eye and said, "Why do good things always seem to happen to you?" Now, I had my share of crap happen in my life, but I understood what she was saying. I had an epiphany in that moment that through choosing to see the world as kind and positive, I was actually creating these little wins in my life. That day, I became more intentional about manifesting my life. You can too.

Fill the blanks in this sentence as many times as you need to feel complete.

Today I will be _____ *and attract* _____ .

Today I will be _____ *and attract* _____ .

Today I will be _____ *and attract* _____ .

Today I will be _____ *and attract* _____ .

Today I will be _____ *and attract* _____ .

Today I will be _____ *and attract* _____ .

Today I will be _____ *and attract* _____ .

Today I will be _____ *and attract* _____ .

Today I will be _____ *and attract* _____ .

Today I will be _____ *and attract* _____ .

Today I will be _____ *and attract* _____ .

Today I will be _____ *and attract* _____ .

Keep going if there is more!

Affirmation:
"I am what I wish to be, do, and have."

Day 5

You make a difference every single day simply by being you. Not the roles you play, or the image of who you think you are supposed to be. The true, beautiful, and authentic you ripples out and touches lives.

Three things for which I am grateful...

1.
2.
3.

Regardless of who you are or where you have been, there is beauty and love in you.

I spent most of the first four and a half decades of my life trying to hide who I was because if you knew who I really was, you would run for the hills with your hair on fire. That's because I didn't love or accept myself. I had no clue who my Authentic Self was, and I was terrified to look. I was living so many lies on top of lies that I didn't even know the truth. The lies were built around denying the trauma of my first two decades and pretending I was "normal." That none of that had happened and I was, "fine." I'm fine. I had two beautiful babies and they became my world. The most unconditionally loving creatures I had ever known. I lost myself in being their mother. Selfishly filling my cup with their lives. This is very dangerous and completely unhealthy and unfair to them. It's called burying the wounds with outside distractions and people and hoping no one notices the cracks and fissures erupting along the way. Smoke and mirrors, baby. Nothing to see here. By my own choosing, I was a Stepford Wife. Just less polished. When I woke up to who I am and looked at myself clearly, I was not surprised to see the defects and shadow side, but I was astounded by the love and beauty that was actually within me all along. It was exhausting to live in denial. I let go of the roles I play and embraced my capacity for love and healing. For myself and for others.

Describe your true, authentic self. Not the small self, but the fully present and empowered you. How will your Light ripple out today? Take the time you deserve in really owning this empowered view of you.

_____

_____

_____

_____

_____

_____

_____

_____

_____

_____

_____

_____

_____

_____

_____

Affirmation:
"Today, I touch lives in a positive way."

𝕯ay 6

If there is no python or bear in your midst, your fear is not real. Fear is an illusion that can run (or ruin) your life. Consciously choosing courage and living from the heart will deeply change your life.

Three things for which I am grateful...

1. _____
2. _____
3. _____

The fear response manifests in fight, flight, freeze, or fawn (pacify or appease). We all tend to have a dominant go-to response when confronted, challenged, or triggered. Anger is always masking fear. Ask yourself, is the fear real? Will you die on the spot if you are honest and clear? If you ask for your needs to be met? If you do not receive approval?

The first time I remember engaging in a powerfully healthy conversation after both parties triggered each other, the person said to me, "Wow, what just happened really triggered me. Are you open to walking through this so I can understand what I am feeling?" I thought WHAT? That's the most incredible (and weirdest) thing I have ever heard. And I said, "Yes." He then proceeded to tell me how what I did reminded him of his ex and he was triggered and I realized it was not personal. Then I got to tell him the reason I did it, which was very different, and what he did that triggered me too. Two adults. We put aside the fear of abandonment, imperfection, confrontation and walked through our stuff and out the other side. Our connection was deeper after that and it's a perfect example of how if we know that nothing is personal, we have nothing to fear.

List the fears that have habitually robbed you of joy.

Are these fears real or are they thoughts of what could happen?

How much of your conscious life do you spend thinking fearful thoughts and worst-case scenarios when you could be living and creating your life?

Since you have realized that your fears are illusions, are you willing to give them up now? If not, be willing, to be willing. When fearful thoughts come in, just notice them in a new way. Don't give them power.

Your mind doesn't know the difference between an actual event and an imagined one. It believes it's real. Shift your thoughts away from the ones that cause you angst or stress and focus on other things. Cleaning, a book, writing, bathing, dancing. If you say, "Cancel, cancel, cancel," you can stop the loop.

*A*ffirmation:
"I allow my mind to rest and I live from the heart."

Day 7

The Universe will whisper. Then it will speak. Then it will shout. Then it will run you over with a Mack truck. Listen early and you can consciously navigate your life.

Three things for which I am grateful...

1. _____
2. _____
3. _____

You are receiving an extraordinary amount of information all day long. Far more than your ancestors did or even your parents. Scientists say it's about 74GB per day and 5% more each year. We cannot possibly pay attention to and process all of that information. It amounts to around 16 two-hour movies a day. Your mind works constantly to filter out and pay attention to what is important for survival and what matters to you. You can actually train your brain to pay more attention to the higher-level information coming through by setting an intention.

One day, I decided that it would be a good idea to go horseback riding by myself. I had always ridden with a pack of other riders on the trails in a national forest. It was extraordinary to navigate the wilderness with these gentle but very powerful animals. A communion of (wo)man and beast. On this particular day, it was gray and cloudy and had been raining with some thunder and lightning which had let up. I chose the gentlest of the horses. I had the thought that it was probably not smart to go alone. The first whisper. I ignored the thought, saddled her up, and started in the paddock. There was a little clap of thunder and Marshy jumped a tad and I thought maybe I should just go around a few more times and call it a day. The second whisper. I ignored the thought and I headed out the trail. I saw a man on the trail, waved and said hi.

He reached up while holding his white plastic grocery bag in his hand, to say hello. My normally steadfast and gentle horse was freaked out by the killer plastic and wheeled around so fast that I was left hanging in the air like a cartoon character. I didn't want to break my wrist or collarbone, so I tucked in and landed on my humorous on the edge of the dirt-packed trail curb. My arm snapped, thus, the Mack truck. The upper arm cannot be cast, I had to keep it in a sling and lie in bed for two months while depending on the kindness of others, as it healed. If I had listened to the first whisper, I could have avoided much. The gift? I have listened to most of the whispers ever since.

What whispers have come your way?

What current thoughts most require attention?

_____
_____
_____
_____
_____
_____
_____

What action steps will you take today?

_____
_____
_____
_____
_____
_____
_____
_____
_____
_____
_____

Affirmation:
"Today, I listen to my intuition and take action."

Day 8

Every single person is equal to one another, neither above nor below. As such, each of you deserves a life of freedom without apology or explanation.

Three things for which I am grateful...

1. _____
2. _____
3. _____

Until you address and change your beliefs and thinking around who you are and what you deserve, the acceptance and abundance that is your divine right will elude you.

Given all that I learned and lived through my first quarter of life, it is no surprise that I suffered from low self-esteem. I was constantly seeking approval and acceptance from others so that I could feel average. I didn't even want "better than", I simply wanted to not feel "less than". The problem is that self-worth is an inside job meaning that I could seek outside validation all I wanted but it would never fill the black hole in my gut. Doing the work to realize I am equal, deserving, and worthy was the only thing that set me free.

Exercise

Take a deep breath. Close your eyes and imagine yourself in the center of the room. Surrounded by people. In this first scenario, imagine what it feels like to need their approval. How does it feel? Does it actually fill you up? Make you feel good? Some will like you and others will not. Do you need anyone's approval to feel worthy in the world? Hint: There is no amount of approval from the outside world to fix or heal you.

Now close your eyes and take another deep breath. See yourself in the center of the same room. Surrounded by people. Only this time, you need no one else's approval but your own. Breathe that self-acceptance in. Embrace the flaws. Embrace the magic. Feel the power of self-love enveloping you. Feel how grounded and whole you are.

How do you feel standing there, confident and sure?

_____

_____

_____

If you truly believed you are as worthy as anyone you know, what would you stop doing for acceptance and approval?

_____

_____

_____

_____

_____

Knowing that they cannot give you worthiness, are you now ready to release the need for anyone's approval? They cannot fill the missing piece you perceive. Only you can.

Affirmation:
"Today, I accept that I am equal and worthy."

Day 9

You are the captain of your ship. Use the tides and the winds to carry you effortlessly to what you desire. Flow easily in the direction of the current that is aligned with your highest good.

Three things for which I am grateful...

1. _____
2. _____
3. _____

It's within your power to choose your experience. One of the most dynamic things you can do is get out of your own way.

For years, I was a wife and mother. I helped my husband with his businesses but made sure that I was there at all times for my kids. I wanted to be that mom. The one that did better than mine. The one that was creative and cool. The one that made no mistakes. I once said to my mother-in-law, "I want to be the perfect mom." She did the kindest thing she could have done, she laughed out loud then said, "Good luck with that!" The other moms would say, "When I come back, I want you to be my mom" because I made life fun and creative. But when my older child hit puberty, the fantasy came crashing down. Before, I was just flowing and going with it because it was easy. When my older child started having challenges, I fought it tooth and nail. I didn't want her to suffer or to put herself in opposition to life in any way. Why? Because it scared me. I didn't understand it. I wanted to control it to keep her safe and me from feeling discomfort or fear. I began to fight the trajectory of our lives. To row upstream. I did not have the necessary tools to navigate the rapids and I kept trying to turn my boat around and go back to where life was easier. I was fighting the current and it was exhausting and painful. When years later, things were illuminated and I understood that I couldn't help, control, fix or change my beautiful child, I realized she had her own boat now and it wasn't up to me. That I had to flow in my life and honor the flow of hers.

Life does NOT have to be hard.

Have you ever noticed that some people seem to just have it easy? That everything seems to "magically" come to them? While others are struggling? Describe a situation where you have noticed this and share your insights as to why this might be.

_____

_____

_____

_____

_____

What are your beliefs about how the world treats you? Details both the positive and negative beliefs.

_____

_____

_____

_____

_____

_____

_____

_____

_____

_____

Do you see that you have the power to turn your boat from paddling upstream or in the rapids and gently go with the flow?

Where can you stop struggling?

Is there something you are making harder than it needs to be in your life?

What could you do instead?

Affirmation:
"I am captain of my ship and I flow with the tides of abundance."

Day 10

Everything that has happened to this point is perfect. Do not judge your life as good or bad. Know that you would not be the person you are without all of the experiences you have had.

Three things for which I am grateful...

1. _____
2. _____
3. _____

Shame and guilt are the lowest human consciousness vibrations as calibrated by David Hawkins. They are usually the first feelings triggered when we make a mistake or remember a time where we felt bad about ourselves or our lives. We are the only creatures on the planet that re-traumatize ourselves again and again with our big brains thinking and rethinking on an endless self-defeating loop. The cheetah is not worried about its spots. They simply "be" without self-consciousness. That's the goal for us. To simply, lovingly "be." Be unconditional love which is halfway to enlightenment.

I had a beautiful teacher, Mrs. Ellerbrook. She taught art and I was such a lost teen without a great deal of support, so her attention to me and my ceramics was like a salve on a deep burn. I worked harder and longer than anyone in the room to please her. I gained at least a small level of self-esteem from being really good at something. Finally! Sometimes, she would give us an assignment with general guidelines and the piece would come to me in my dreams. When she asked me if I had been photo logging my work for college acceptance I was dumbfounded. I had so much unprocessed shame. I was a walking wound. I felt I was an imposter posing as a talented artist and now was the time I would be found out.

She came to my little one-bedroom apartment where my sister, my mother, and I lived, and she photographed everything for me. It didn't matter that I didn't get into the college. It mattered that someone cared. It mattered that I tried. Later, I went on to UCLA and created eight-foot sculptures and art that processed my pain and my joy. Throughout my life, that foundation of creativity and support has motivated and propelled me in everything I do. You do not know whose life you will change by getting out of your own way and sharing your kindness and love.

What experiences still haunt you? This could be anything.

Can you now find and acknowledge the positive attributes that happened as a result of your challenges? For example, strength, resilience, creativity, empathy? List the challenge and the gift and how it has enhanced your life. Specifically, how it turned out to be for your evolution and advancement?

Ask the Universe to help you let go of any residual attachment to the story about what happened and set yourself free.

Affirmation:
"Today, I ask the Great Spirit to remove all shame and guilt. I am free."

Day 11

When you stop trying to control yourself, others, or conditions, you take flight. It's in the surrender to life's thermals that you will rise.

Three things for which I am grateful...

1. _____
2. _____
3. _____

You will always know you're in fear if you try to control situations, people or things. You do that so that you will feel better, by being in control. Remember, you came here to love, not collect the most toys or accolades. Knowing this, it's easier to shift from fear and control back to love and acceptance. You are the only one you can change.

When my younger child became a teenager, I was parenting her from fear. The struggle in today's world is real. But my fear was based on nothing that was happening in the present moment. It wasn't even based on her behavior. It was based on the past. Of the things I experienced as a teen, fear of the things I witnessed my older sister go through, fear that I was not enough as a mother, fear that I needed to control life so that my child would not feel pain. She was bullied. I wanted to kill the perp. Or cover her in bubble wrap. The unconscious fear was that if she felt discomfort or pain, I would too. And I wouldn't survive it. I had to control our worlds. And then God laughed. The wise being that she is, my kid said, "Mom, I love you. I am not my sister. I am not you. I am not doing weird stuff. I am fine. I am where I say I am. I am doing what I say I am doing. Stop." Inherent in what she said was, stop being afraid, stop trying to control me, just relax, trust me. Live and let live.

**List a few ways in which you attempt to control or manipulate
people, places or things when in fear.**

**Instead of immediately trying to control the situation or person,
what could you do instead, to feel better?**

List the tools you could use and which ones you will implement the next time you feel in fear or out of control.

Example: Counting to 10, breathing, meditating, pausing when agitated and checking in with yourself. Come up with a few of your own too.

_____

_____

_____

_____

_____

_____

_____

_____

_____

_____

_____

_____

_____

Until it becomes your default behavior, you may have to put a post-it on the mirror or computer to remind yourself of your new commitment to yourself.

Affirmation:
"Today, I surrender and trust the journey."

𝔇ay 12

What we tell ourselves is what we become. I am whole. I am love. I am joy. I am complete. Rinse. Repeat.

Three things for which I am grateful...

1.
2.
3.

In the Four Agreements, Don Miguel Ruiz says, "Be impeccable with your word." It changed my life because he talked about being kind and integrous with others. More importantly, he said, "Do not speak negatively to yourself."

I interpret that as, speak your truth, be kind to others but most of all be kind to you. Words have deep power. If you speak negative words out loud, not only do they harm through their meaning, but they harm energetically as they cling to the objects around you. Imagine what happens when you have incessant, negative inner dialogue. There was no one on planet earth who put me under a microscope and picked me apart the way I did. The power of thought and word cannot be underestimated.

You are going to do something now that will be your agreement with yourself. Use it to remember who you truly are. Write a positive statement describing your essence when you are empowered. The twist is that I want you to use words that are in fact you, but you may not believe or own them. My affirmation or contract with myself is "I am a loving, courageous, self-respecting woman." I created this at the age of 25. They were states of being that I wanted to embody and eventually grew into. Another example is "I am a vulnerable, powerful, loving man."

Try it out on a loved one and see if they "get it." Don't use too many words, you want to be able to access it and repeat it easily. The words may be things you may not fully feel now but want to solidify. If fear is a companion, include the word courageous and so on. Once you have it, say it out loud several times and tap on your chest at the same time, anchoring it into your body.

Write it down on a Post-It. Put it on your mirror, steering wheel, refrigerator, wallet or computer so that you will be reminded, and know that is your truth. Move the post-it around so that object permanence doesn't kick in and stop you from noticing it.

What feelings came up as a result of this exercise?

Affirmation:
"Today, I accept all of me and continue to grow."

Day 13

Ancient wisdom tells us that it's the story you attach to the events of the past that still causes you suffering. The event or trauma was real in the moment, but it has long since passed. Knowing this, you have the power to move beyond those thoughts.

Three things for which I am grateful...

1. _____
2. _____
3. _____

Do you have thought loops? Do you go back over events and try to rewrite the ending? Things couldn't have been any different than they were because they happened as they did and accepting that will help you flatten the energy on it and let it go. Everything that has happened is part of your evolution.

After a particularly intense interaction with my older daughter many years ago, I kept replaying what happened over and over again. Then I looped back through her entire life trying to see where I had gone wrong, what had I done, what had she done? Then I looped forward and thought through the 'What ifs?' What if she goes? What if she comes back? What if she's unhappy her whole life? What if she's not in my life? What if she is? My merry-go-round brain tortured me daily. Fortunately, a wise shaman said to me, "You and your daughter had a contract in this life. This part is done. Let it go. The relationship will be what it is meant to be, but for you to engage with and have attachment to your stories about what you think it should be will only make you miserable. She is an adult and you are not responsible for her choices or her journey." I truly had to let her go and honor that her life and experiences were exactly what she came to earth to understand.

For a trauma bond this deep, it took years of learning and healing to truly become neutral and let go. Waking up to and letting go of how I was torturing myself by looping back to try and fix the past set me free to a very big degree. I realized I was not a victim of her or my past unless I chose to be.

You will know that you have healed your attachments to your stories when you are no longer triggered.

Write out the story that still returns to you. Are you willing to let the thought loops go? Once you have finished it, find a beautiful tree and tell the story one last time. Let the emotion come and let it move through you and out. One week later, add to the journal entry your current/new truth around the story? Don't revisit the details of the story, just your current feeling about it. Less sad? Neutral?

Meditation Exercise

You can't change the event, but you can change your perception or perspective of it. To do that, go back in time as the healed version of you and see it through the eyes of love and understanding.

To do this, find a comfortable, quiet place. Settle in, take three deep slow breaths through your nose. Now, imagine seeing the event you wrote about as a movie. Watch it with non-attachment, view the movie and the characters with neutrality. Notice what you did not see before. The hurt, the fracture, the motivation, the courage, the fear. If you can now see it from an adult, healed perspective, it no longer has a stranglehold on you. It simply was. You can do this a few times to really flatten the energy on it.

Affirmation:
"Today, I let go of thoughts that do not serve me."

Day 14

If you stay in the past, you become trapped and limit your possibilities. You are a warrior. A survivor. You are not what has already happened. You are the story of now.

Three things for which I am grateful...

1. _____
2. _____
3. _____

What you tell yourself about past events is such a deeply impactful habit. It's time to further challenge that old story.

My childhood was ridiculous. I began as a princess in my own mind. Clearly dropped into the wrong family by the stork. Started life in a new tract home with a Cadillac in the driveway. I had beautiful, intelligent parents who had the requisite 2.3 children. The American dream. Soon it became a relentless nightmare. Life went to crap very quickly. We moved a lot. My older sister's mental illness and drug addiction manifested in her teens affecting all of us. My parent's alcoholism progressed rapidly. Divorce happened. Financial insecurity ensued. My little sister and I dumpster-dived for food... thinking it a grand adventure. Thirty years later, at a high school reunion, I realized I was not the only one living with a carefully crafted facade. Several people confessed their truths, abusive fathers, drunken mothers, secrets I had no idea they harbored. They too had suffered. We always think we are alone and because of my own secrets, I felt like a phony, less than, damaged and unworthy. I carried these thought burdens through much of my life. Thinking I was bad, fractured, and undeserving of love. What I came to understand is that all of these experiences made me who I am. There is no one I have met at this point whose story can shock me.

I have empathy and compassion for people because I have worked hard and come to accept myself and my journey. I had to understand that I am not the things that happened. I am the Phoenix that rose from the ashes. The survivor and the goddess all in one.

What is the current story you tell yourself about who you are as a result of your collective past?

I now see that the strengths that I gained from navigating the past...

The lessons I learned about my resilience are...

What I'm specifically willing to let go of regarding the past is...

My new story is... (it doesn't have to be your reality yet, but it will be)

_____

_____

_____

_____

_____

_____

_____

_____

_____

_____

_____

_____

_____

_____

_____

_____

_____

_____

_____

𝒜ffirmation:
"Today, I see that I am whole and powerful."

Day 15

There are moments, seconds even, throughout the day where there are decisions to be made, big and small. What to eat, where to go, whom to marry? Most people are on autopilot, and they keep getting the same life over and over. Like Groundhog's Day.

Three things for which I am grateful...

1. _____

2. _____

3. _____

The subconscious rules about 90-95% of your actions. Many of your thoughts and actions are guided by things you don't even realize are buried within you. Since you don't come with a "How to be a Whole Human" manual at birth, it's all trial and error here on planet earth. It really does need to be enough that you are doing your best and your best will change as you do. You are like an onion with so many delicious layers. One layer is not better than another. It's simply what is revealed in the present moment that can be transmuted.

Being on autopilot means living from your unconscious mind. I have always said, "If you don't confront and heal what ended your relationship, you will find the same person, with a different face." I kept attracting men who did not respect or honor me in my 20s. They all had very different faces, races, and socio-economic backgrounds. I thought I was a victim of these, "horrible humans." I had no father after 11, no brothers, no male role models at all so I hadn't a clue that men are just people with different plumbing. When I realized that I was the common denominator and I was the one dishonoring and disrespecting myself, I knew I had to learn how to be a healthier person. To heal myself because it wasn't them, it was me. Another layer was revealed, where I realized that I needed to own my worth and "stop accepting crumbs and calling it a banquet."

I invite you to become more mindful and conscious in your day-to-day life. Come off autopilot in your life. Decisions you make today, affect your tomorrow.

Whatever choice comes to you today, stop, get quiet, go inside and ask the question: What choice is for my highest good? Then write what comes to you.

The second and very powerful step is taking action on what comes to you. What action steps make sense to you for the above?

Affirmation:
"Today, I choose well and mindfully move through my day."

Day 16

Things are not broken. You are not broken. Things may be breaking apart or breaking down but that's so that they can reform in a new and powerful way.

Three things for which I am grateful...

1. _____
2. _____
3. _____

There is an extraordinary practice called Kintsugi. It is the Japanese art of repairing broken pottery by fixing the parts that broke or, "imperfections," in a unique way. They mix the lacquer with powdered gold that fills the cracks as a uniquely beautiful tribute to the history of the object—not something to hide or turn away from.

I spent most of my life in pursuit of perfection. Another way to say that, is I spent my life in pursuit of control so others would admire and accept me. Maybe it was because I was raised on Barbie. She was perfect. She was smooth, her legs were 100 feet long and she never blinked or got mascara smeared on her face. I thought you would only love me if I was smooth, thin and perfect. It was a frustrating and unattainable illusion. Don't get me started on Ken. This was written before the movie came out. That's how iconic they are.

To be clear, perfection as a Soul is already achieved. There is nothing more for you to do or be in order to be perfect; however, the pursuit of perfection as a human being is unattainable and will constantly make you feel like you are never enough.

Embrace the cracks. Fill them with gold.

What in your life feels like cracks are forming and it's breaking down?

How will you re-form this in a more powerful supportive way, cracks and all?

Who in your life can/will support your process? What do you need from them? Go ask them. Give them the opportunity to show up for you and deepen the emotional intimacy.

Affirmation:
"With all my imperfections, I am beautifully whole."

Day 17

Human beings are the most resilient, adaptable creatures on the planet. This absolutely means you.

Three things for which I am grateful...

1. _____

2. _____

3. _____

"Whoever is stiff and inflexible is a disciple of death. Whoever is soft and yielding is a disciple of life. The hard and still will be broken, the soft and supple will prevail." – Tao Te Ching

I once did a parenting course just before my first child was born. It was called, *"Faith Parenting the Miracle Child."* It was the first time that I truly saw how rigid I was in my thinking. *Controlling* may be another way to describe it. I came from such chaos that I came by the coping mechanism of control innocently. My children weren't even born yet, and I wanted to control the experience of my children. I wanted to make them happy and protect them from harm and pain. Putting them in a giant protection ball didn't seem out of the realm of reasonability. *Faith Parenting* said to create a safe environment and love them. Also, let them fall. Let them explore. Let them become who they are meant to be, not what I think is best for them. I should have taken the course every year because parenting, by its very nature, demands flexibility and adaptability. It's like they spend their days thinking of new ways to throw you off. We do this to ourselves as well and the most important parenting you will ever do is for your own inner child. To acknowledge, support, heal and love yourself unconditionally will in turn, change every relationship.

Back to the Tao Te Ching, yielding, or agility and adaptability, are superpowers. Where do you need to be less rigid (hard) and more adaptable (soft) in your own journey? With others?

_____

_____

_____

_____

_____

_____

_____

Give examples of how you can be more flexible with yourself, people, places and things.

_____

_____

_____

_____

_____

_____

_____

Affirmation:
"I am flexible and adapt easily."

𝔇ay 18

Everyone has a unique and powerful sojourn. The Hero's journey is yours. You are the mortal turned warrior who goes on life's adventures, encounters obstacles, wins victories, and becomes transformed.

Three things for which I am grateful...

1.
2.
3.

The most extraordinary people that I have met are forged in fire. You have come up against obstacles in the form of situations or relationships that have challenged you to become more. To find your inner power and strength. The adventures, obstacles and victories do not have to be dramatic or spectacular. They are your experiences and they are perfect for your awakening and evolution. You may be in the process now. Trust that you will come out the other side stronger, happier and more resilient. Master Class says, "The hero's journey is a common narrative archetype, or story template, that involves a hero who goes on an adventure, learns a lesson, wins a victory with that newfound knowledge, and then returns home transformed."

My hero's journey could be considered my entire life. There is a story within the story that I will share. I was going through menopause while my older child was going through a complicated adolescence. I fell off my horse, broke my arm, tore up my leg, gained 100 pounds, several close friends passed away, it was the Great Recession and we lost our house. Oh, and my mother was dying. That's not all of it, but it's enough for you to get the point. This perfect disastrous storm brought me to my knees. It triggered the trauma I had been carrying (and pushing down) from childhood for decades. It brought me to a crossroads.

Do I keep pushing forward and endure the pain, or do I get help? Do I face my demons or go down with the ship? Where to start? I call what I did the spiritual shotgun. I did not one thing, but many. First, I made a decision that was to begin my spiritual transformation. Second, I created a healing team. I made the decision to change my lifestyle and thus my life story which led to an entirely new life.

Now it's time to tell your Hero's Journey. What happened in your life to challenge you?

_____

_____

_____

_____

_____

_____

_____

_____

_____

_____

_____

_____

_____

_____

_____

_____

_____

_____

_____

_____

_____

_____

How did you overcome it to transcend to the next level of your life?

_____

_____

_____

_____

_____

_____

What are the most important things you learned about yourself?

_____

_____

_____

_____

_____

Do you see how you are indeed the hero of your story?

_____

_____

Affirmation:
"I am the hero in my life."

Day 19

Choose to play. Be childlike today. Tap into that innocent joy and the magnificence of who you truly are.

Three things for which I am grateful...

1. _____
2. _____
3. _____

Choosing joy is not only possible, it's mandatory for a life of bliss. Remember, it takes exactly sixty seconds for your brain to talk you out of a good idea so if you choose to think or do or be something that brings you joy, act on it right away.

Several years ago, as a year-end bonus, my business partner suggested I fly to Big Sky, Montana and stay at his mountain retreat. After emerging from my hero's journey a couple of years prior, I had decided to say yes to life. Not to argue my limitations, so I said yes to the offer. I invited my friend and her fiancé. Up to that point, I had been a once-a-decade skier. My friend was a black diamond snowboarder and frankly, physically, a badass. I took lessons and I learned to ski that day. We also snowshoed. The most memorable, most joyful memory was when we took a running leap into four feet of virgin snow and made snow angels. I hadn't done that since I was a child. We laughed before, during and after. It was a lovely reminder of what it means to be childlike and fully committed to being alive.

What will you do today to bring the feeling of joy? Go out into nature, skip, do laser tag, listen to music, paint, play video games, sing or dance as if no one is watching? What activates your bliss? Now you have sixty seconds to get up and do it if possible. If it is something that takes planning, then you have sixty seconds to get the plan made!

Write down the activity you chose and how you felt before, during, and after.

Affirmation:
"I am joy."

Day 20

What you focus on grows. You are drawn directly to what you put your attention on and vice versa. Therefore, what you make your focal point will determine your experience.

Three things for which I am grateful...

1. _____
2. _____
3. _____

In coaching, I often use the analogy of the race car driver. At 200 miles per hour, if the driver is looking at the safety wall, where will the car go? That's right, crash! When riding a horse, if you turn your head, the horse will want to go that way even if they can't see what you're looking at. That's how powerful this concept is. When you focus on not having, you are lacking. When you focus on the abundance of your life, you feel rich because you choose to see the wealth you have attracted, not what is yet to come. Being able to direct your focus will bring into view the positive aspects of your relationships, home life, friends, experiences, purpose, and journey. You will find a new level of empowerment and happiness in this simple practice.

Recently, we bought our dream house. It has acres and acres of trees and wildlife. We have dubbed it Paradise Ranch. With glass-half-full focus on the positive, everything seems like abundance and bliss. The view. The quiet. The solitude. Nature. A hot tub. The company. What's to worry about? Well, the old me would start freaking out about the what ifs? What if we can't afford it after all? What if we can't get the right insurance? What if we don't like our neighbors? What if it's too isolated? What if we get bored of each other? What if a bear eats me for breakfast? To counteract that thinking, every single day, we look out and say, "We live here. We live in paradise. We are so grateful." Remembering that, "future tripping" serves no one and exists in unrealized fears, I can stay in the moment, in the beauty and really appreciate what is true right now.

If you are in the future or the past, you are missing the magic of the present moment.

Since what you make your focal point will determine your experience, where will you shine your focus light today? What feeling do you intend to create today with your focus? Tomorrow come back to your journal and describe the experience of your intentional day versus a day in the past, when you just let life happen on its own, with no direction.

Affirmation:
"I focus on the positive."

Day 21

What you say to yourself is so powerful that it becomes the difference between you living life as average, or extraordinary.

Three things for which I am grateful...

1.
2.
3.

Dr Masaru Emoto, a Japanese scientist, documented experiments of the effects of words and thoughts on water molecules. He studied the influence of such words as love, gratitude, evil, disgust, thank you, peace, symphony and so on. The positive words created perfectly formed symmetrical molecular structures while the negative words caused marked deformations and discolorations. This is a water molecule! Can you imagine what your words do to others? More importantly, the words you say to yourself create your entire experience so if you are bashing yourself on the daily with negativity, it becomes difficult to truly live your potential.

I used to say the most demeaning, horrible, belittling things to myself. I felt I was fat, ugly, undeserving, tacky, and poor. You get the idea. If I dropped a cup or spilled things, made any mistake at all, it was an opportunity to hurt myself further with internal and external words. I also got to be right about the negative self-talk I had developed through my life. See? I can't even watch tv without spilling. Or I should have checked my tires before two of them went flat. Just the ability to practice everyday care and feeding of being human seemed to elude me. Who could love me? I was such a mess.

As I began to do, think and absorb a different way of being, that all changed. I began to wake up to how self-defeating and untrue so much of my thinking was. The truth is that you and I are love itself. We are deserving of love. We have every right to love.

Begin to notice your automatic inner thoughts. Uniformly, we are the hardest on ourselves. How do you speak to yourself? What is the running dialogue?

That subconscious chatter must be retrained. To help change it at the subconscious level, you are going to create a Vision Statement for yourself. A "contract" if you will. It must be positive and contain things that are true but that you want to enhance and "own." It should incorporate your passion, your purpose, the things that make your life compelling. Start by jotting down value words that resonate with you. Passion, unconditional love, integrity, courage, connection, etc. Then play with it until it fits you to a tee. Remember that it is the feeling, a powerful emotion, associated with your personal vision, or contract, that will manifest the embodiment.

Here's the formula:

CVisualization + Feeling = Manifestation

Examples:
- I am (you can use the same formula as my contract above).
- "I'm awesome."
- "I live a powerful life of purpose and example, inspiring others to live their most alive lives."
- "I inspire people everywhere to be healthy and whole through my teaching."
- "I lead my company with courage and passion such that we manifest powerful change."
- "I make a difference simply by being unique and innovative.

Affirmation:

(Insert your Vision Statement)

Day 22

Everybody gets to choose.
And we are not responsible for what others may decide.

Three things for which I am grateful...

1. _____
2. _____
3. _____

Each being coming into this life gets to choose their experience.
YOU get to choose your experience. Every single day, we make
thousands of choices. Most of these are not conscious and
deliberate choices. If you think for a moment that you are not the
agent of change in your life and that life simply happens (to you)
then you are operating from a place of disempowerment.

Pickleball is a perfect microcosm of life. Any sport would do, but
this is mine. I get to choose my experience every time I step onto
the court. Like life, there may be people you interact with that
you might not like or agree with. It's how you interact that is the
choice. You may come up against people who are more skilled,
better, quicker, mean spirited, driven by anger or have
competitive natures. They could be there on a lark and
completely free of internal dialogue, happy and free. The myriad
of mirrors available to you is astounding.

Several months ago, a man who shall remain nameless, slammed
a ball so hard and so fast it was nearly invisible. That's not
unusual, but my reaction was. It zoomed past me and I got
triggered. I took it personally. I was like a three year old with a
foul mouth and I whipped my head around and said, "F**k" you!"
My regret and remorse was immediate. I was mortified. Here I
am, a paragon of virtue (in my own mind) and I totally lost it in a

rude and graceless manner. I ran over to the net and I said, "I am so sorry. That is not who I want to be in the world and it has nothing to do with you. Can you forgive me?" His eyes got big with surprise and he had a gentle, crooked smile on his face and we shook hands. He was the one with grace. He seemed unphased, but I am not thrilled about my reaction. I had the awareness to examine what happened and then intend a different experience in that moment for all games going forward. My competitive nature, my old need to win and my sense of fairness got triggered big time. From that, I got a chance to choose who I wanted to be in the future. My biggest learning was that regardless of who I play, I'm there to get exercise and have fun. I don't have to be the best and he/she is not a big meanie if they play hard. If it's not fun for whatever reason, I can shift my attitude or step off the court. We choose how we play the game of life.

Think about a time when you behaved in a way contrary to who you wish to be. What happened?

_____

_____

_____

_____

_____

_____

What got triggered?

_____

_____

_____

_____

What were the mirrors?

_____

_____

_____

_____

How would you prefer to handle it in the future?

_____

_____

_____

_____

What are your new choices to bring you the peace and freedom you desire?

_____

_____

_____

_____

_____

Affirmation:
"I live life by choice."

Day 23

You are the creator of all things through your thoughts. Choosing your stream of consciousness will curate a potent life.

Three things for which I am grateful...

1. _____
2. _____
3. _____

Nothing exists without thought. What you are thinking is true, because you believe it is true. What you think is happening, is what's happening. Without knowledge of the power of thought, you become victim to all the thoughts you have been told as if they were the truth. It's time to take hold of your awareness.

I don't mean to throw mom under the bus, God rest her soul. However, she was by far my biggest influence and this is about your healing, I'm sure she would be okay with me sharing this. She once said to me, "All men want one thing." I believed her and attracted that into my life. She said, "Money doesn't grow on trees." I therefore believed that there is scarcity. She said, "You have to finish everything on your plate, there are starving kids in Ethiopia." I thought I had to finish every bite on every plate, ignoring and pushing down my self-trust and intuitive eating.

This led to a lifetime struggle with my food and weight and a lot of unraveling regarding men and money. I came to my beliefs innocently, as did you. As did she. But now it's time to heal them.

What are three limiting beliefs you have?
For example: "I don't have enough education." "I'm not attractive enough." "People don't see me." "I'll never make it."

These are thoughts that have turned into beliefs that get in the way of your abundance and purpose. Remember, the ONLY thing limiting you are the habitual negative thoughts, beliefs and projections that need to be cleared and replaced with truth.

After you have your three, in a quiet space, bring to mind your most limiting belief of which you are aware.

When was this belief born? Did it start even earlier?

Now challenge it, is it even true? Why is it not true? Present the evidence. Write it down.

Example:

"I'll never have enough money."
This is not true because my needs have always been met. I now know there is not enough money in the world to make me feel secure from the outside world or make me happy. I can always find ways to attract more money.

You have been accepting your beliefs as truth for years, yet they originated somewhere else. Society, media, parents. Stop letting those run you.

Take some serious time here and detail why your most limiting beliefs are flawed and incorrect. If you have figured out where they came from, notate that as well and "return them to sender." Give them back. They were never yours to begin with.

Now rewrite the truth here using this mantra shared with me by my magical yoga teachers:

_____

_____

_____

_____

_____

_____

_____

_____

_____

_____

_____

_____

_____

_____

_____

_____

_____

_____

_____

_____

_____

_____

> ## *Affirmation:*
> "I lovingly release myself and others from past hurts. I am free and they are free to live an extraordinary life."

Day 24

Believe in Magic. It's all around and within you.

Three things for which I am grateful...

1. ....

2. ....

3. ....

Meditation helps access the quantum field of possibility. It reduces the stress hormone, cortisol. It lowers blood pressure. Brings peace. Allows creativity to come through. The positive effects are endless and have been enjoyed for thousands of years. In this society of doing, it is counterintuitive for us to honor and give importance to being.

Stillness is the pathway for mindfulness. The ability to empty your mind of the clutter through meditation even for a moment is very powerful. Simple, but not always easy.

I became aware of meditation as a practice back in 1984. I didn't start meditating regularly until 2014. Do as I say, not as I did, Grasshoppa. I wonder how those 30 years would have been different had I actually followed through? The benefits of meditation over the last decade have been profound. I am a kinder, more present, happier, more grounded human being. I have peace and clarity that were not part of my vocabulary before. When I get tired or agitated or afraid, meditation resets, restores and renews my wellbeing.

What has stood in the way of a daily meditation practice for you?

Do you think you need to do it perfectly? Millions of people benefit every day, why not you?

How will you make a beginning? Put a stone, talisman or crystal in your hand. Concentrate on the feel, the temperature, the shape. Thoughts will sneak in. Acknowledge (don't judge) them and go back to the stone, or the guided meditation voice. Allow your body and mind to reset, restore and renew. The human body and brain need to heal in this way to be fully available and healthy.

---

*A*ffirmation:
"Today, I let go of the chatter and find peace in the present."

Day 25

No regrets. No, "should haves."

Three things for which I am grateful...

1. _____
2. _____
3. _____

It's time to remove the words, "I should" from your vocabulary. When you get caught up in the "I should haves," of your life, you are making yourself wrong, second guessing yourself. Everything that once happened is in the past. It's time to embrace what is and lighten up through the process because returning to the past is only good if you acknowledge it, learn from it and move on. "I should," will lower your vibration, stunt your emotional growth and enslave you to your negative thoughts.

If I didn't know that everything happens for my benefit and for my highest evolution, I could live endlessly in the "should haves" of life. I should have trusted myself. I should have chosen differently. I should have had more kids. I should have waited to marry. I should have had no kids. I should have never ridden a horse. I should have saved more money. I should have gotten that other degree. I should have moved sooner. I should have traveled more. I should have appreciated being in the now. I should have, should have, should have. How disempowering. How sad. Shifting into gratitude cures just about everything. As my friend Jack said, "Gratitude is the bridge to joy." It raises the vibration. It shines the light on what matters. It allows forgiveness and acceptance.

It's usually true that for each should have, there was a fork in the road. You could have chosen one but chose the other. If the other was chosen, your life would have played out in a different

way. Again, wondering and "shoulding," only lowers your vibration.

What are the three biggest "should haves" with which you minimize yourself or your life experience? For each of these, write how you now see that it was the perfect choice in that moment with the knowledge and tools you had. After each of these write, "I now see and accept that this was perfect for me and I am grateful."

Affirmation:
"I release these thoughts with love. I did and will continue to do my best."

Day 26

Being "woke" is not an insult. It's a state of awareness that is only for the brave.

Three things for which I am grateful...

1. _____
2. _____
3. _____

The process of spiritually awakening means that you become aware of your own divinity. Once you know you are a spiritual being having a human experience, that cannot be unknown. It sounds simple, but it is akin to being a Spiritual Warrior in a 3-D world that wants to hang onto its collective 2-D ego. In other words, you will encounter resistance within and without.

I remember thinking that being awake to the spiritual nature of all that is and how I alone am responsible for my experience was both exhilarating and freeing. Learning to truly "see" people and their motivations and truths was uncomfortable. I had changed, but not everyone around me had. People often hate change and if our friends and family are used to us dancing life's dance in a certain way, they will not be happy if we change the rules by waking up, healing, or learning healthy boundaries.

Remember, when you become healthier and change how you interact with people, they may balk. They may become uncomfortable and long for the old, possibly, dysfunctional you. Do not let their need to stay the same and keep you in a box, dictate your journey. Honor that they have their own path and timing. But more importantly honor that your time is now.

When your transformational journey makes others uncomfortable or you encounter resistance in the form of people wanting to stay angry, negative or small, what will you do to protect and continue your spiritual momentum?

*A*ffirmation:
"Today, I accept the journey of awakening without judgment of self or others."

Day 27

Negative self-talk will sabotage your success. Notice without judgment how you speak to yourself. Is it positive and empowering? This is the single most compelling thing you can do to create immediate internal change.

Three things for which I am grateful...

1.
2.
3.

This topic is so important that it will be addressed a few times in this book. It is woven into everything you do. Waking up to what you say, when you say it and being able to lovingly acknowledge and shift your thoughts to more supportive ones is imperative for your journey of self-acceptance and self-love.

For me, the most overwhelming theme of my negative self-talk as a young woman, had to do with worthiness. That I didn't deserve happiness, success or love. Why would anyone I wanted, want me? And if they did want me, what was wrong with them? My ego had big ideas about what I deserved but the shadow side of the ego sabotaged left, right and center. Who do you think you are? It would ask. Here was a big one, "If they knew who I really am, they would be disgusted and leave me." I remember meeting the drummer of a rock band. He would come into the restaurant where I worked and request my table every time he was in town. I knew his order by heart and we always flirted. He had huge black 80's rocker hair. So kind and gentle. I knew he had a little crush on me and certainly enjoyed the attention. It was West Hollywood so you could throw a rock and hit an actor or a musician, so I didn't think much of it.

One day, he came in with a friend who was extremely clean cut. He introduced us and said he was this guy's limo driver. I said, "Cool." Next time he came in, he was with another guy with giant black hair and I said, "Now this guy looks like he belongs to you." He laughed and he said, "Yeah, actually, we're in a band together." I said, "That makes sense. What's your band called?" He said, "Kiss." Without skipping a beat, I said, "Huh, I think I've heard of them," and walked away. When I came back, he asked me out. I still didn't think he was who he said he was, but I said yes anyway. The truth was that I didn't let it go beyond a few dates because I knew how unworthy I was. I knew I would not be able to keep the cool, funny, confident facade intact for a relationship with an international star. I knew my inner demons of negativity and unworthiness would win. So I stopped it before it could become anything that I could destroy. Talk about, "upper limiting" yourself. He later died of a brain tumor in his 30's. I would have loved to have known him now! It was shortly after this time frame that I did an emotional intelligence training where they said in no uncertain terms that I could make a difference as one person, and I believed them. It changed everything. I began to speak differently to myself and believe I was worthy of a good life. Timing is everything. It wasn't a spontaneous process to love myself, it was relentlessly conscious. And it was to be a lifelong journey.

Write down the negative thing(s) you say to yourself when you are stressed or make a mistake.
For example: I can't believe I did or said that! I'm stupid. I hate myself. I'm a misfit, an imposter, an idiot.

Take a moment and ask yourself, is any of it true?

Hint: NO. Self-awareness is the first and greatest step toward emotional intelligence.

Now, take each of the things you say and examine them with no judgment. Are you stupid? "No, I said a stupid thing. That doesn't make me stupid." Making a mistake is just that, it doesn't make you a mistake.

Pick the negative thoughts apart. Just because you've always said them doesn't mean they are true or that you need to keep that negative habit. You innocently picked them up along the way, now you can consciously let them go.

Prove the lies wrong. Use the evidence of truth.

***A*ffirmation:**
"I do my best and I'm enough."

Day 28

Everything that happens is a moment of learning. Don't judge what happens. Get curious about the, "Why?"

Three things for which I am grateful...

1. _____

2. _____

3. _____

Everything that happens, happens FOR us. It deserves to be said many times. That means that no matter what happens, whether positive or negative, if approached with an open mind to how it is for you, it becomes part of the fabric of what's next. Fighting the challenges in your life takes up too much energy. Accepting them as challenges and dealing with them without emotional attachment, rather than trying never to have any, will help you see and navigate them more clearly and effortlessly.

When I went into private practice with my Executive Leadership and Strategic Life Coaching, I called a friend. A very accomplished trainer and coach. He was happy for me and he said, "I don't know why, but would you like to sit in on the leadership workshop I'm doing next week?" I had decided that no matter what I would try and not let fear interfere with my life. That everything happens for a reason and though I didn't know why either, I said yes. I thought it would be boring, but I also didn't want to be ungrateful. During the workshop, I was inspired. It was exhilarating to be in the workshop and remember what being of service looks like. It turns out that he and his associate were booked to do a series of workshops around the world for the studio's culture change. I thought, "This is what I want to do." I jokingly said, "Hey, my passport is up to date if you ever need extra help." We both chuckled.

Two months later, he called and said, "Were you serious?" Circumstances had changed with the associate and he needed me to help him run the workshops both in LA and Argentina, Australia and the UK. What a whirlwind of YES! If we put our desires into the universe and listen for the response, magic can happen.

Sometimes the situation is not as positive as this one. Sometimes the "why is this happening" has to do with a challenge. Either way, you can learn and grow from it if you practice non-attachment and non-engagement in the outcome.

Think of a situation or dynamic in your life where you would like to examine the why?

To get to the why, ask what is this here to teach me?

What are the possibilities? That very question means you are in learning mode. Circumstances are neutral. Our reaction is often not neutral because we don't think we want it. Coming from curiosity is a beautiful way to neutralize negative emotions. From here, you can find the nuggets or transformative treasures as the result of every situation.

Write it out.

Now think of another situation that has troubled or inspired you.

Ask yourself what have I learned? What is this here to teach me? If you can begin to have this line of inquiry be your default reaction, your life will sky rocket!

Affirmation:
"Everything that happens has the potential to enhance me in a positive way."

Day 29

The only way out of fear is through it. To get through it, you have to remember that no matter what, if it's not a grizzly bear at your door, or a tiger in your tub, then your fear is an illusion.

Three things for which I am grateful...

1. _____
2. _____
3. _____

Let's look at the fear of not BEING enough. I'm not enough. I don't have enough. My relationship is not enough. There is not enough food. There is not enough love. I don't know enough. I am not enough as a sister, daughter, mother, father, brother, or son. I'm always falling short. If I'm not enough, I will not be loved, people will leave me, and I will die alone under a bridge pushing a shopping cart.

Do you see how fear can expand and spiral all based on a false premise? Fear always drills down to survival. The truth is that there is plenty for everyone. It's a world of plenty. The Universe has always had your back. The only shopping cart you need to worry about pushing is at Costco or Whole Foods.

By design, fear is addressed several times in your coaching journey. Why? Because it is so pervasive and foundational in keeping you a victim in your life. Everyone has fears. *You either have fears, or they have you.* If you acknowledge your fears and process and manage them, then *you have them.* If they run your life and the quality of your experience, then *they have you.*

What are you afraid of? How much does your fear interfere with your aspirations?

Is the fear actually happening or is it imagined in the past or the future?

Ask yourself, what am I avoiding by continuing to hold onto the fear of this thing? Failure...or SUCCESS?

Affirmation:
"I release my fears and live powerfully in the present."

Day 30

Blessings come in unexpected ways. They are all around us. The butterfly. Sunlight through the leaves. Moonlight. A smile. Lift your eyes and you will see.

Three things for which I am grateful...

1. _____
2. _____
3. _____

Be curious and alert to the present moment.

One day, my friend Camille and I were driving around in her open jeep. Through the streets of Beverly Hills, no less. Our 20s are all about "Who am I?" I was struggling with this and she wanted to shift my experience in the moment. She drove down one of the tree lined streets that was named after a type of tree and pulled over next to, you guessed it, a giant tree. The sun was beaming through the leaves changing them to various translucent shades of green. She leapt out of the jeep and ran over to the biggest one she could find and hugged the stoic and patient tree. It was the most joyful and genuine thing I had ever seen anyone do. She waved me over and told me I had to hug it too. I didn't hesitate because I didn't want to be a killjoy, though I wasn't sure what I was supposed to feel. Then, I felt wonder. Wonder that I actually got out of my own way and did something so spontaneous. Wonder at the realization that I didn't have to follow the expected rules of decorum all the time. Wonder that I didn't even care who saw me. Wonder at the power of nature that was all around me and I had never noticed in this way. Wonder that strangely, I did in fact, feel better. Forever, when I drive those toney streets, I think of Camille and of magic. She changed me in that one blessed moment with a simple act of love and friendship. She taught me that blessings are all around us waiting for us to simply stop and engage in them.

Looking around your environment right now, what blessings do you see, hear, smell, sense?

_____

_____

_____

_____

_____

What blessings will you receive from the universe today? Abundance? Connection?

_____

_____

_____

_____

_____

_____

_____

_____

_____

_____

Affirmation:
"Blessings come to me easily and effortlessly."

Day 31

There is no light without the dark.
It's an impossibility, so embrace and learn from your shadow side.
It is neither good, nor bad. It simply is.

Three things for which I am grateful...

1. _____
2. _____
3. _____

There is a place where a lot of us live...until you don't. It is called the, "I don't know what I don't know," place. This is the most dangerous of places for you because oftentimes, you are unaware of how you are being perceived or affecting others with your words and behaviors. They are called blind spots. You may be unaware of the negative attributes or "shadows" you carry. If you are oblivious, you cannot change. But if you Wake Up, you can.

When I was about 27, ironically during my Saturn Return, a stage where one crosses a significant threshold of maturity and enters the next stage of life, I did an inventory of myself. I took a long hard look at my life and what I was doing or being that was perpetuating the chaos and disharmony. I had no idea I had so many character flaws. I was shocked by the self-assessment and astonished that I had any friends left at all. With all that, who in the world would put up with me? Self-righteousness, control, judgment, gossip, low self-esteem, victimhood, entitlement, just to name a few, had been my constant companions. They were my learned coping mechanisms from years of survival. They were also my shadows that I had pretended did not exist. Yet, there they were, influencing everything I did, every relationship - business and personal. Until I woke up to these parts of myself, I could not clear or heal them. I first went to shame, then relief. I now had a choice.

A shadow cannot exist without light. Think of you in a dark room. You turn on a floor lamp and suddenly you can see your shadow behind you on the wall. Courageously shine a light on your inner shadows through consciously being self-aware.

What are your blind spots?

What are your defects in thought or behavior that keep sabotaging your happiness?

Go deeper. What are your go-to behaviors that keep you from the light?

Once you have been honest with yourself:
Ask the Universe to help you let go of those behaviors and thoughts.

In time, you will notice how you have been relieved of the things that no longer serve you.

Affirmation:
"I shine my light brightly and proudly."

Day 32

You are not a victim.
You are a decider.
You are a chooser.
You are a victor.

Three things for which I am grateful...

1.

2.

3.

You are the boss of you. You and your spiritual truth. Not a victim.

Coming from poverty and a broken home, there were rules of living that I missed the boat on. I was literally flying by the seat of my pants. I have read that the prefrontal cortex is not fully formed until the age of twenty-five. That happens to coincide with a decision I made. A choice that changed my life. I was working at a restaurant when another very handsome man came in with a bunch of joyful humans. I waited on their table and they were so happy, positive and kind that I asked them, "Who are you people?" They were from a personal awareness (emotional intelligence) training that was taking place down the street. The head guy, we will call him Mr. Handsome, invited me to come to a guest event. I had that whisper that said this is important. I asked more questions and found out that there was going to be another training the following month. My friend Camille, the tree hugger, had also done the training and encouraged me to check it out. This one serendipitous night changed the course of my life. In those training sessions I was taught the rules of living I had missed: accountability, personal power, choice, making a difference, empathy, self-worth, mindfulness, leadership, the power of positivity. It was to become the foundation for my becoming in this lifetime. It was the shift from VICTIM to VICTOR. That is your opportunity here. Whether it is church, a workshop, this book, a movie, there will be many of these vehicles of possibility that may present themselves over your lifetime. You will see and hear them when you are ready. You will move into being a victor when you choose it.

What is the unaccountable victim story you tell yourself today?
"I'm too fat, poor, old, young, unattractive, broken?"
"I'm alone, judged, forgotten?"
"My parents sucked and that's why I am the way I am?"
"The thing that happened to me, defines me?"

Tell your victim story.

Now, go back and tell it again from the point of view of the survivor, the victor. How you survived and now thrive. You get to decide when and where you become the victor. Yes it happened, and it sucked, but this is a different moment in time, and you get to choose if it will continue to define you.

_____

_____

_____

_____

_____

_____

_____

_____

_____

_____

_____

_____

_____

_____

_____

_____

Affirmation:
"I thrive in victory."

𝔇ay 33

Vulnerability is a superpower. To be vulnerable, you must peel back the mask of the role you play and let it go. If only for moments at a time. Until it is the norm.

Three things for which I am grateful...

1. _____
2. _____
3. _____

Here's the funny thing about masks. We think we are fooling people. That they cannot see the chinks in our armor. The pain or uncertainty behind the facade. Maybe not all people can, but if you are here doing this work, you are likely hanging out with perceptive and conscious people who can and want to see the real you.

When I married at 28 years old, I started wearing pearls and making people call me Mrs. Lerner. I was, after all, a respectable doctor's wife now. I was presenting what I thought people wanted to see. And what I thought would finally get me the respect and approval I always craved. The mask of propriety and gentility was laughable. I was a wild woman on a motorcycle, not June Cleaver. My venerable (and also wild) mother, who often came up with some really good ones, said, "Since you got married, you lost your sparkle." Talk about seeing through the mask. The sparkle was who I was as a Being. That connected wild, creative, crazy, beautifully flawed me. My authentic self. My husband never asked me to change. He didn't marry me for my pearls. He's the one who gave them to me. Who was I trying to fool? What was I trying to gain? Clearly, I was inadvertently and inaccurately running from my own magic - not realizing that being me was not only enough but necessary.

You cannot get to true connection through the mask you wear.

Describe your mask (tough, controlled, powerful, rich, mean, fragile, the clown, the elite, the tough, the prince/princess, the designated patient, the academic, the hippie). For me, I wore it thinking I could get love, approval and respect. All things I needed to give myself.

What do you think you will get by wearing your mask?

What do you think the mask is protecting you from?

Now that you think about it, do you still believe that people can't see through it?

Once you identify the masks, you can let go of them. The
Authentic You is enough.

Affirmation:
"Who I am is real, authentic and true."

Day 34

Authenticity means to live your life according to the knowingness and alignment of your inner being.

Three things for which I am grateful...

1. _____
2. _____
3. _____

I sound woo-woo here, even to me. "Knowingness," and, "alignment of your inner being." What does that even mean? We all have our little self, the ego. We have the big Self, the Divine you or inner being. Ego is a necessary aspect of being human. It creates distinction between you and others. The ego lives in the five senses and thinks it is in charge. The ego is not bad, it is a necessary aspect that assists in navigating this 3-D world but if the ego is in charge, sustained ecstasy and joy are unobtainable. The ego thrives on comparison, competition and otherness. Having said that, it is possible to co-exist and recognize when the ego takes over. You will know by how you feel.

My ego used to show up as competition, need for perfection, acquisition, and fitting in. Now it shows up most around relationships. *Nothing is personal. We all have our own spiritual journeys. Everyone is doing their best. Other people's behaviors can be triggered by long ago installed buttons. Change takes time.* And the most important one: *everything happens FOR me, not to me.* If I believe all of the above, then I can recognize when my ego steps in to mess with me. For example, for years after our conscious uncoupling, I kept thinking that I was responsible for my ex-husband's current experience of life. His happiness. His failures. His successes too. I wanted him to find the right match and fall in love.

In short, I would cause myself grief paying any attention whatsoever to his life. It wasn't my business. It was just my ego. How in the world was I responsible for another being? A grown ass man. With a formidable will and intellect? I was judging his life and wanting him to be happy so that I could be happy. Just ego. When I think of him now, it's with love, friendship and non-attachment. Mostly. Still a work in progress.

When you understand that who you are is not your ego, the roles you play or your identities, but your divine inner self, you will be able to get grounded and centered and access that part of you.

Describe how and when your ego shows up.

Now, take a moment to breathe and connect to your inner self. Not the ego self you present to the world. From this place, describe who you truly are. Go all in. If this is difficult, it's ok. Maybe use the eyes of someone who loves you. Imagine them describing you. The true, loving you. All else is smoke and mirrors.

If you are not used to loving and accepting you, this may have been hard but it will get easier as you move into the truth. That you are unique and worthy of love and loving.

*A*ffirmation:
"I am aligned with my divine inner being."

𝔇ay 35

Everything that happens is for your benefit.
If life is uncomfortable or feels negative, it's simply an
opportunity to see where you are out of alignment
with your truth and where you need to course correct.

Three things for which I am grateful...

1. _____
2. _____
3. _____

People balk at this one until they really examine it. In hindsight
and with an open heart and mind, you will always be able to see
how everything that has happened, happened for you. If negative
things have happened, I am truly sorry for your pain. Living in
that story will only cause extended pain. Being able to see the
courage, the insight, the strength that you are because of your
past—this will set you free.

My parents came to me and my sister when we were tweens and
said they were getting a divorce. I was thrilled. Now the fighting
would end. I could go live with my dad and live happily ever
after. The reality was that we three girls went to live with my
mother who had not held a job since before they married. She
was ill-equipped to support us. We ended up on food stamps and
wiping our butts with newspapers when we couldn't afford toilet
paper. My older sister's mental illness was in full swing and my
mother's drinking was exacerbated by the divorce. It wasn't what
she thought it would be. We moved back from Ohio to California.
Life felt unsafe, confusing, dangerous even. How was this FOR
me? Well, I thought I was a victim for so many years. My princess
fantasy trajectory was smashed, and I ended up in an ordinary,
even subpar life. I escaped home, completely self-supporting, at
age 17.

I seemed old and wise at the time. But I was a child without support or tools for living. In hindsight, it was for me because I learned self-reliance, excellent work ethics, strength, resiliency, compassion for others, and after years of dysfunction, I learned (through pain) that I needed to make some hard choices and choose another future. I will forever know that the Universe has always had my back. And it drove me to heal and in turn become a healer. To help others get beyond their circumstances and thrive.

Are you willing to see now how the things that happened, happened for you?
Rather than relive the negative in detail, create a list of each event whether it is family, siblings, loss, or an infringement on your boundaries and rights, with one word or phrase. Then next to each, write:

> What I learned about myself is...
> What I will avoid in the future because of my experience is....
> I know that I can handle anything because...
> The Universe has always had my back. I know this because...

Affirmation:
"Everything happens for me."

Day 36

Course correction is a viable and desirable option.

Three things for which I am grateful...

1. _____
2. _____
3. _____

Just because you or a part of your life has always been a certain way, does NOT mean that change is not possible. You have every right to change your destiny.

A person can get so dug in and committed to being right about a past belief or choice that they cut off their own nose to spite their face. Brutal, but so specific and true. It means thinking you are punishing the other person by withholding or doing something that actually punishes yourself. This is not only ineffective but exacerbates and inflates the pain. Here's another one, "It adds insult to injury." Like doubling down on yourself instead of realizing you need to shift or admit when you're wrong or throw in the towel (bad relationship) for your own good.

Let's say you want to lose weight. You have a meal that was bigger than planned or a food on the red list. Do you say, "That's okay baby, you'll do better tomorrow." And then course correct and make a plan for success? Or do you say, "I'm a f-up, I can't believe I did that!" and then "I might as well eat a pizza." Or perhaps you have been cultivating a relationship and you crave connection, emotional intimacy and companionship but you keep looking for flaws and reasons to run? Or you are needing to connect so badly that your energy scares the other person off and you have created the lack of what you desire? Do you course correct and say, "Wow, I'm doing it again. What is actually true? Why am I judging this person? Am I coming on too strong? Am I making assumptions?" Oftentimes, we create what we fear and then get to be right about our fears.

What do you want to change today? How will you begin that change?

_____

_____

_____

What do you want to change this year? What are the steps?

_____

_____

_____

_____

What do you want to change over the next five years? What are the steps you will take?

_____

_____

_____

_____

_____

*A*ffirmation:
"I embrace change and transformation."

Day 37

Gift yourself with moments of silence today.
Quiet the "crazy," or the cacophony.
It's in the silence that the messages
of your inner wisdom can be heard.

Three things for which I am grateful...

1. _____
2. _____
3. _____

For some of us, the quiet is scary. The old thoughts may come
sneaking (or blasting) through. For some, it's peaceful and a
welcome respite from the tens of thousands of pieces of
information coming at you from all sides. For others, it's what
they have been shielding themselves from their whole lives.
Running from the silence and their true or false thoughts of
themselves.

I started listening to the silence about twelve years ago. Before
bed, my younger daughter and I had a ritual. Under the twinkly
lights in her room, we would meditate. With crystals in our hands,
we closed our eyes and waited. The strangest thing started to
happen. Allie would ask me questions, and I would ask the
Universe and tell her what was coming through. It was just a fun
thing to do until we realized that what I was seeing was actually
coming true. Meeting people, who and when, what they looked
like, and the successes and connections coming. We were pretty
blown away. For years now, I've been asking the Universe yes or
no questions. I know the answer that comes from stillness can be
trusted. Of course, in the beginning, I had no idea what I was
doing and later learned what was appropriate to ask and how (no
free will questions). A pendulum is a great way to do this.

Throughout the last decade, I have been quieting the crazy every single day with meditation. I recalibrate, rejuvenate and reset. Through this process, the crazy has become a distant, negligible hum, a non-issue. In order to do this regularly, I honor the importance of this practice by putting it on my calendar every day. I begin by thanking the Universe for this amazing body and life that has stood the test of time. I ask my Guardian Angels, White Buffalo Medicine Woman and Athena, to restore my body to God's perfection. And if I have a particular injury or illness, pay particular attention to that. To remind the trillions of cells to do their job the way they know how to do. I ask for help in cutting the energetic cords to any negative energy. Then, I ask for guidance for whatever is going on in my life at that time — and go still. All of this happens in a matter of moments.

Exercise

Ease into stillness. Start small. You can use music, meditation videos, apps, drums, dance, walking, breathing, even guided meditations targeting what you want to work on. Youtube has a plethora of choices

What, if anything, scares you about the inner silence?

_____

_____

_____

_____

_____

_____

_____

_____

_____

What methods have you tried in the past? Which one worked best?

Can you let go of the need to do it perfectly?

How will you tap into silence today?

$\mathscr{A}$ffirmation:
"I am comfortable in the silence."

𝔇ay 38

It's not your job to control other people. Surprise! - and you're welcome. You have zero control over other people and that's the good news. The only one you can change is you.

Three things for which I am grateful...

1. _____
2. _____
3. _____

As you accept that you have no control over others, don't panic. It wasn't working anyway. It really is the good news because it takes the pressure off of you trying to control anything, anyone, or any place outside of you. Stop avoiding your inner work by pointing at others as the source of your unhappiness. Strangely, as you change your perspective and attitudes, the people around you magically seem to change as well.

Relieved? Confused? So often people think, "If that person would just do this or that, then I would feel better." Beneath all impulses to control, is fear. Fear of not getting your needs met. Of being seen as less than. Of being revealed, unhappy, or wrong. Parents are guilty of this all the time. I saw my children suffer in different ways. I was told to get them tested and out of fear (and hope) I did. They came back as having ADD. This is not a bad thing, it's just neuro diverse. At the time, I thought it was bad and I was going to fix it so that they felt better (and I suffered less from their suffering). We tried tweaking their diet and getting rid of processed and sugar foods. We tried hypnotherapy, acupuncture and regular therapy. We tried calming the environment and improving their sleep. None of it really made a difference and truly for one daughter, there was a lot more going on there that would reveal itself later. As a last resort, we tried medications.

I suppose for some people, that may work well. I really have no judgment for others but for us, it didn't work. If I were to do it all again, with my current knowledge and level of healing, I would have done a few things differently. In some ways, I did a stellar job, in other ways, I would love a do-over - said nearly every parent who ever lived. But as I have said, everything happens for us. And them.

***For those with this diagnosis, some of the most creative and extraordinary people in history have had ADD/ADHD. It is what it is and my hope for you is to work with it, not against it, and find your peace and your superpower within it.

How have you tried to change things as a way of trying to manage your fear and feel better?

What did you think would be better as a result?

Do you now see that you have no control over those things?

Why is that a positive thing?

Who do you most try and control in your life? Why?

Do you see that you don't actually have control over others?

Why is that a positive thing?

Who, what, and where will you surrender your need to control in the future?

_____

_____

_____

_____

_____

_____

_____

_____

_____

_____

_____

_____

_____

_____

_____

_____

_____

_____

_____

_____

_____

_____

Affirmation:
"Happily, the only person I choose to control is me."

Day 39

Confidence does not come from without. It comes from within. Believe that who you are is enough.

Three things for which I am grateful...

1.
2.
3.

Another word for confidence is self-trust. If you trust that you will always return to your inner compass, your values in any situation, and your clear boundaries, you can trust that you will show up in alignment. From here you will know the best thing to be, to say or to do in any given moment.

I was the weird, nerdy girl from Ohio who was new at a California High School. My clothes were not trendy, I cut and bleached my own hair, and I wiped my nose on my sleeves when I had a cold. We moved often, my family was dysfunctional and there was zero emotional security in our home, so confidence was not my forte. Figuring out how to make friends became a fulltime job. I felt like I was scrambling, always. I thought, "If only I had money, a normal family, I was thin, I looked right, then I would be confident and happy." I call it the as soon as syndrome. As soon as these things line up, the red carpet of life will magically unravel and the paparazzi will recognize my magnificence. It took years of life and inner work to realize that confidence is an inside job. I actually had the house, the husband, the money, the body, the whatever and I realized that yes, all of this really is lovely but none of it makes me whole. Wholeness, personal power and a true sense of self is not about stuff or looking good or blending in.

You don't need anything outside of you to make you whole. Believe in you and realize that every single other human is just trying to figure their stuff out too. Have the confidence to own your unique contribution to the planet.

How does/will it feel to live life from a place of confidence and being enough?

_____

_____

_____

_____

Finish this sentence.

I am confident and people want to know me and spend time with me because...

_____

_____

_____

_____

*A*ffirmation:
"I am confident in myself."

106

Day 40

Everything is your teacher. It's up to you to figure out the lesson and integrate it. Otherwise, it will come again, and again, and again in different forms or faces.

Three things for which I am grateful...

1. _____
2. _____
3. _____

Relationships will always be the greatest indicator of personal awareness and a lovely way to know where you need work. The lessons of self-care, selflessness, connection. The lessons of avoidance or need for conflict are just some of the facets that will rise for healing. I dated men who were basically different versions of my father, over and over. Charming, handsome, funny, intelligent, dysfunctional, alcoholic, weak, philandering, and wonderful. He was all of those things, so it felt familiar to my childhood self. I was asked to be married by two different men on the same day. That's a whole other story and maybe it will show up later, but I had to choose. I loved them both. One felt exciting and familiar in his chaos, and the other felt like a soft place to land in his kindness. That he would be a good father and husband. Seems like an easy choice, yes? It took me three months and a list of pros and cons to choose the good man. The truth was that there was a third choice of choosing neither and trusting that I would not end up alone with a horde of cats. All choices bring lessons and he was the right choice at that time. How do I know? Because that's the choice I made. I knew where the other relationship would end up. This one, I took a leap of faith and the marriage was a thirty-year segment of my life with two remarkable children and many ups and downs. What would I have chosen if I knew then what I know now about trusting the Universe and choosing from empowerment and not fear? We will never know but making peace with our past is paramount to the joy of our now.

Think about your life. Are the people that you have dated or drawn into your orbit the same person with a different face? That's not random. You are the common denominator so take a look at the qualities (negative or positive) that you are attracting.

Think of the 2-3 most influential or important relationships in your life right now. You could also look at your last 3 relationships.

Are they healthy people? How does that look and feel?

_____

_____

_____

_____

Are they narcissists, abusers, loving, angry, door mats, people not in their power, kind, co-dependent, givers, takers, unavailable, avoidant, anxious, or available?

_____

_____

_____

Are you locked in an unhealthy dynamic or are you marveling at how functional and healthy they are? Be honest.

_____

_____

_____

Do you see a pattern? _____

What is it?

_____

_____

_____

_____

_____

_____

What do you learn from this?

_____

_____

_____

_____

_____

_____

_____

_____

You cannot change what you do not acknowledge so congratulations on your honesty. It is the beginning of the shift.

*A*ffirmation:
"I am honest and open."

Day 41

Where there is love, there cannot be hate.
Where there is love, there cannot be lack.
Where this is love, there cannot be fear.
Where there is love, there is you.

Three things for which I am grateful...

1. _____
2. _____
3. _____

Remember, any other emotion than love is an indicator that you need to shift your focus and your vibration. That you are off-center of your True Self. Recalling who you truly are and that you came here to love will bring you back to balance. The easiest way to shift to love is to remember who you are and what you are grateful for. It's why in this practice, we begin every day with three gratitudes. It creates an instant vibration shift which in turn, allows more love.

In my early adult years, I was an angry tornado. What I have come to realize is that all those early years of trauma, lack of psychological or physical safety and turmoil, left my body with the somatic scars I would carry within myself for years. I managed my emotions as best I could with the tools I had. Until I was able to clear the trauma from my body, I was reactive. I was overly sensitive. I was in fear... a lot. Of course, when I got triggered, anger would be my reaction because the fear beneath it required a release. If I was alone, I would slam the kitchen cabinet door so hard that it fell off the hinges. I used a staple-gun and duct tape to fix it before my poor husband got home. I never took that anger out on my future children in that way, but I now know that epigenetically, they had it or they could feel it even if it didn't manifest outwardly. Energetically, they could feel it. I ran around with my Stepford Wife mask of perfect mommy all the while dying a little each day with the effort to appear, "normal." Proud that I never raged at my children like my mother did and yet the sleeping volcano of emotional turmoil was ever present beneath the surface. It took a lot of food to quiet that beast.

Be aware that masking your pain and your trauma only seems to work. Others can see and feel your pain. As you move through this series of self-reflections, day after day, week after week, commit to clearing all the, "invisibles." Commit to setting yourself free from things you may not even know are running you.

Note: If you have never tried EFT (Tapping) or EMDR, I highly recommend it. And remember, your life timing is perfect for you because you only know what you know when you are ready to know it.

Exercise

Embrace your feelings. Each emotion has a vibration. The emotion will tell you instantly if you are in alignment with love or not. Then you can shift.

NOTE: You may not be able to immediately know what you are feeling. Do not get frustrated. Or do. But you can make a beginning.

Ask yourself:

Do I have any sensations in my body right now?

Where are they?

Does it feel tight? Does it feel stressful? Does it feel warm?

What feelings are associated with those sensations?
Play with it. Feelings are not facts, but they are indicators. They are breadcrumbs to knowing your level of happiness and when it's time to shift.

Make a list of what and whom you love.

How does it feel to love them?

How will you show up as love today?

---

*A*ffirmation:
"I am love."

ᛞ℣ay 42

Gratitude is where all healing germinates.
If you are thankful, you acknowledge the bounty.
If you acknowledge the bounty, you are in abundance.
If you acknowledge the abundance, more of it comes to you based on what you are emanating into the world.

Three things for which I am grateful...

1. _____
2. _____
3. _____

Being grateful, or thankful, is the gateway to joy. In fact, it is a shortcut to happiness. I once saw a clip on the life of Dr. Wayne Dyer, who was a force for positive change and enlightenment for decades. Definitely an expert on living a purposefully good life. What struck me most is that every single morning he put his palms up and this was his prayer, "Thank you, thank you, thank you." That's it. That was the daily keystone moment for everything that followed throughout his day.

When I was sandwiched between caring for my mother, my older sister, and my daughters, I didn't see a whole lot for which to be grateful. I was so low, depressed, it was hard to keep my head above the waves. Yet the pain of that time period was what drove me to awakening and ultimately to my destiny. For all of humanity, it's been a stressful ride these past few years and I'm sure many people were loath to find anything for which to be grateful. And yet, there is so much.

List all the ways your life is currently abundant. Do not qualify or minimize. Start with the abundance of love or connection and drill down on the details. As you acknowledge your abundance, more is on its way!

_____

_____

_____

_____

_____

_____

_____

_____

_____

_____

_____

_____

_____

_____

_____

_____

_____

_____

_____

_____

_____

_____

Affirmation:
"I am abundant in all areas of my life."

𝔇ay 43

Human connection comes through communication.
We communicate in many different ways.
Most of them are random and unconscious.
A look. A touch. A twitch. A sigh.
Imagine if we train and focus that communication
for the highest good of all.

Three things for which I am grateful...

1.
2.
3.

Connection is critical for happiness, longevity, and exploration of your world. Think of a newborn baby, the caregiver needs to connect through gaze, sound and touch. The baby learns their world this way. They learn if it's safe or scary. As adults, you learn in the same way, taking cues from the people and situations in your life. If the cues are loving, accepting, non-judgmental and otherwise positive, you will flourish. If they are negative, you will not. Today's reading is not only about the people you surround yourself with, but the cues you are sending out into the world. It's all interconnected.

When you awaken, stay in the beautiful, vulnerable space of renewal and set your focus on your connection and communication with others. Acknowledge that all of the people in your life are in fact, your teachers. When we honor them as such, and choose how we will connect, magic is therefore accessible in every encounter. All the clues are there for you.

I used to look down at the ground when I walked. Afraid to try and connect with others, just in case they rejected me with their eyes. As if they had that power. When I shifted into purposefully giving to others with my eye contact and smile, not caring how it was received, it became an interesting study in human nature. I was not looking to get their approval. I was creating the opportunity to have a connection. It was not up to me how it was received. It was their choice to smile back and feel good, or not. But I got to choose to feel good giving, regardless of their response.

How will you communicate with strangers, loved ones, and yourself, today?

_____

_____

_____

_____

_____

If you encounter an unpleasant person or situation, how will you respond?

_____

_____

_____

_____

_____

Will you remember that nothing is personal? Will you pause?

_____

_____

_____

_____

What would you like others to experience from you today?

Are you willing to let go of negative, mean or vampiric people in your life just for today?

*A*ffirmation:
"I am consciously and subconsciously loving."

Day 44

Intention is a way of guiding your experience in life.
If you do not set an intention for your day,
others, or life itself, will decide it for you.

Three things for which I am grateful...

1. _____
2. _____
3. _____

An intention is something that we are aiming to do or accomplish.
It rises from the rational mind and involves thinking and
choosing the experience we intend to manifest. It is how we
happen to life, rather than life happening to us.

I was married on a typical June day in California. They have
what's called, "June Gloom" where the fog rolls in for most of the
morning. By now, I was about three years into my journey of
awakening. I had the knowledge that all kinds of things could go
wrong on a wedding day. That I had to let go of control and
expectations and that whatever would happen on our big day was
going to be fine. I was not self-aware enough to really see my
control issues as a hindrance as yet. I knew that I had orchestrated
and controlled every single detail: the bridesmaids' earrings,
make-up, hair, and dresses, right down to the flowers and food.
What I had no control over, was how it would all turn out. I
consciously intended that the day was going to be perfect, no
matter what. I decided to let go of control regarding the
ceremony and party and try to enjoy myself. It didn't matter that
the photographer charged me 10 times what I thought (my bad),
or that the wedding singer saw her ex-boyfriend at the wedding
and ran out the door after the first song, or that my future sister-
in-law had a glass or two of wine mixed with jet lag and passed out

with her head on the table. None of it mattered because I had set the intention to not ruin it for myself by focusing on imperfections and things out of my control. If only I had carried that into the rest of my life from that moment!

Blessedly, it would become the norm to not look for drama. To live in acceptance and surrender. To seek peace rather than extremes. But it took time and effort.

How do you intend to live life today? Conscious or unconscious? Connected or unconnected?

What is the experience you intend to create (joy, abundance, connection, adventure, chaos, understanding, drama, love)?

Describe what it will feel like to live with intention.

_____

_____

_____

_____

_____

_____

_____

_____

_____

_____

_____

_____

_____

_____

_____

_____

_____

_____

_____

_____

_____

_____

Affirmation:
"I create my own reality."

𝔇ay 45

Trust, my love.
Everything that has or ever will happen,
is for your evolution.

Three things for which I am grateful...

1. _____

2. _____

3. _____

You are being asked to trust your life and this process. There are certain themes you may have noticed are repeated here in this book. The story you tell. Not being a victim. Letting go. Living in love, not fear. They are so fundamental to your being able to go to the next level of joy and happiness, that you will be asked to examine and clear these again and again.

I was eight months pregnant with my first child when we decided it was a good time to buy our first house. We looked and looked. We found the only house we could possibly afford in Pacific Palisades, CA. It's a toney area near the beach and it was a severe fixer upper. During escrow, the inspector explained why the homeowners had accepted our offer. The support beams were compromised, and the foundation needed to be fortified. The owner was an inventor who had jerry rigged and re-wired the house, so the electricals needed to be replaced. The roof was leaking so it needed a new one. It hadn't been painted or maintained in decades. Instead of one type of metal, the plumbing was patchworked with several and needed to be replaced. Though we were devastated because we couldn't afford the house because of the repairs, we probably dodged a bullet. We didn't have the capital to fix a doorknob, let alone renovate the entire house. I was sad because my ego really wanted to live where the rich (happy) people lived. Then, I thought, I would be happy. We moved on and bought a house in an area called The Valley that as a family, we would inhabit for 19 years. It was two miles from the schools the girls would need for the first 10 years of their education and in an area where we could build a good life. I am very clear that not getting the first house happened for us, not to us. Think, "This or something better" so that you leave room for the magic you can't yet see.

To move toward your evolution, pick out another limiting belief or story about what has happened in your life and describe it.

Now go back and look at it from the "Condor's view". Looking at it from a distance gives you a different perspective. From there, can you see how each player has their own interpretation and experience? Their own truth about the same event?

_____

_____

_____

_____

_____

_____

_____

_____

_____

_____

_____

There is no right or wrong in this telling. Be open to a new interpretation of your part, and theirs, and set yourself free with the knowledge that you are not trapped in your old views or their limitations. You can now honor that their story is theirs and you do not need to make them see your truth for it to be valid.

*A*ffirmation:
"I see things clearly."

Day 46

Everyone in your life is a mirror. It will take courage to look, but you can't heal what you won't see.

Three things for which I am grateful...

1. _____

2. _____

3. _____

People are our greatest teachers. I once said to my mentor, many years ago, "I can't stand that woman. She just wants to hear herself talk and all she does is complain. Every time she opens her mouth I want to scream or punch her in her cartoon face. Bla, bla, bla, bla, bla." Rather than jumping on board my judgmental pity train and agreeing with me, my mentor said, "I find that usually if someone is bothering you, it is a mirror. There is something about them that's in you, that you need to heal, and she is simply the reflection." I was so angry. Like, seriously? That is not the response I wanted. I wanted her to validate my righteous indignation. I wanted to bond over how awful this woman was. But the truth from my mentor hit hard and stuck. I began to look at every judgment I had in a different light. To check in and see what I needed to address and heal. Including being judgmental. Is it always a mirror?

Yes.

First you look to the present and see where the mirror is and if it's not a direct reflection and you do not find it, look to the past and see where the mirror is. If it's not there, that means in the future, you are going to be presented with the opportunity to engage and heal the behavior. Being willing to change or let go of your own mirrored shadow behavior will literally neutralize your reaction to their behavior. We cannot change others, but they will no longer irritate or trigger you in the same way. It was never about them anyway.

Who triggers you in your inner circle? Where is the mirror?

What tends to trigger you in your interactions with strangers?

How do you wish (expect) them to be different?

_____

_____

_____

_____

_____

_____

_____

Based on the concept and revelation of mirrors, how will you change your perspective and behaviors?

_____

_____

_____

_____

_____

_____

_____

_____

_____

_____

Affirmation:
"I am willing to see my own reflection."

𝔇ay 47

Every human views life from their own unique perspective. Billions of unique perspectives. None are right and none are wrong. They simply are.

Three things for which I am grateful...

1. _____
2. _____
3. _____

If you view your life from one side of your mind's eye, you can see only what is visible from that angle. But If you are willing to deliberately move to another perspective, you may discover an entirely different scenario. This empowers you to choose.

The truth is that you are worthy by virtue of being born uniquely you. This lays the foundation for the truth that your view, or perspective, is deeply valuable. Have you met someone who absolutely needs to be right about their point of view? There is a scarcity mentality in that. Everyone has a unique truth or view. Honor your perspective and your voice by speaking your truth and holding the space for others to do the same. Your experience of people and relationships will change.

I started a podcast years ago. Partly because I needed a voice. What better way to push myself into my own truth, than speaking to people every week who have already done it? I was coaching people and I had a strict walk your talk policy. I won't ask you to do what I am not willing to do. It's one of the reasons I launched it, to overcome my fears. I didn't know how it would go, if anyone would listen, or if it would even matter. I was doing it to help others and in the process, I ended up helping me. I took a two-year break from the podcast when I lost my inspiration.

I moved to a small town where some people surprisingly started listening to them. As a result, they shared their transformative journey with me, and it was exhilarating. It was inspiring. It was a kick in my butt to get back to it. So, I did. You never know how being authentically you will help another. That's not your business. It's your job to just show up and do your best.

How will you view your life and the choices made?

When have you stayed silent for fear of retaliation?

What is the perspective you choose?

Going forward, are you willing to observe all of life with curiosity and respond accordingly?

_____

_____

_____

_____

_____

_____

_____

How do you think that will feel?

_____

_____

_____

_____

_____

_____

_____

_____

_____

_____

Affirmation:
"I live in the present and I choose my experience."

Day 48

When your best intentions go awry, there is always a Plan B. This is the "bob and weave" flexibility that will keep you out of judgment and fear. It means that rather than panic or react, you pause, get curious, and respond to what is actually in front of you.

Three things for which I am grateful...

1. _____
2. _____
3. _____

No matter what is happening in your life right now. Know that it will pass and whatever you are feeling will change and that it's part of life's process to ride it out. I invite your first thought, after YIKES, to be, "I am not sure what's in store for me, but the Universe has always had my back." Panic and worry shuts down the creative, solution finding part of your brain (prefrontal cortex) which means you don't have access to a Plan B. Worry creates no positive results. Breathe, trust the Universe, know that everything is always working out for you. From that point, you can ask, "What next step is in my Highest Good?"

I once had a lucrative executive coaching gig that came to an end. It was a program with a beginning, middle and end – so I knew the expiration date, but still felt bereft afterwards. The people I coached for six months had become a part of the daily fabric of my life. I used my breathing, I reminded myself that it wasn't personal. I told myself to trust that the Universe knew what it was doing for my greatest good. I said all the right things to myself. The things I coach everyone else to do, but I still had to tell my ego to sit down. Ego thinks it's in charge, and it can be, but not if you want consistent peace and joy in your life. A week later, I had moved on and was excited that I could get back to writing this book. And restart my podcast. And posting content. I asked the universe to bring to me what was next for my highest good. The end became a beautiful beginning. Everything can literally be an opportunity.

When you find that you are thrown for a loop, and need a Plan B, how will you interrupt the old reaction pattern and respond with calm curiosity?
For example:
"Hmmm. Interesting that this is happening.
I am amazed that I am staying so positive.
I wonder where this will take me?
I know everything is an opportunity, I wonder what it is?
I think I will meditate and ask what is next for my Highest Good?"

Write it out.

---

*A*ffirmation:
"I am present in the now"

Day 49

Connection is not a mystery. It's in direct correlation to the level you are willing to be open and give of your heart.

Three things for which I am grateful...

1. _____
2. _____
3. _____

The only way out is through. Feel the feelings and allow the healings. There may be some unhealthy people or situations in which you need to protect your heart, but for the most part, living connected to the heart is a boon. Ultimately, you came here to planet earth to love. So, learning discernment and the ability to connect and live with an open heart will bring you bliss beyond your wildest dreams.

I lost my dad when I was only twenty-two. I didn't realize how young that really was. I shut down my heart. I didn't cry for five years and I wore that fact as a badge of honor, as if it was a good thing. Look how strong I am. I don't need anyone. The unprocessed grief was too great for me to fathom. I compartmentalized and pretended it didn't affect me. The goal was to protect myself from loss and pain, or so I thought. The isolation meant all of my relationships were injured in one way or another. I was emotionally unavailable and did what I could to use smoke and mirrors to deflect your love.

My heart was cracked wide open four years later, during the emotional intelligence workshop I stumbled upon. The students were supposed to be in their seats by the time the music ended. If not, you got processed. I was in my seat, but I realized I had sunglasses on top of my head and ran over to my purse to get rid of them. The music stopped and there I stood. In the middle of the room. All eyes on me. After talking to me for a bit the trainer said, "Huh. You must be a real joy to be in a relationship with." I was thrilled that he actually thought I could have one at all. At that moment, I realized how lonely I really was. I vowed to open up in that five-day training and give it everything I had. I knew it was a chance to break wide open and though unsure about what was ahead, I knew that staying stuck and self-protected was no longer an option.

If you try to armor up or shut down to protect your heart, instead tell yourself, "You're safe, I've got you."

Make a list of people or environments in which you wish to be more open hearted.

Write two ways you will stay connected to your heart such that you are able to connect to the hearts of others.

Toxic people breed and breathe toxicity and it is an extreme act of love for you to walk away. Who do you need to stay away from at this time to protect your energy and your heart?

Note: Guided Chakra meditations are a great way to balance all chakras as well as accomplish heart chakra connection in particular.

Affirmation:
"My heart is safe and open and I connect effortlessly."

𝔇ay 50

Do what it takes to change your life because you are the only one who can.

Three things for which I am grateful...

1. _____
2. _____
3. _____

There is an old, old prayer condensed and made popular in the early 20th Century:

"God, grant me the serenity to accept the things I cannot change, the courage to change the things I can, and the Wisdom to know the difference."

I attended UCLA back in the 1980s and finished in 92. It was my dream school. I got good grades in high school but that was relatively easy to do compared to college and I was in culture shock. There were 40,000 "kids" and I felt completely alone. I was such an awkward turtle growing up. Being an adult didn't really change that. It felt like high school all over again. I had no idea how to set myself up to win. In fact, I sabotaged myself. I partied at night and scheduled 9:00 am classes. I swung my false bravado around like a sword and wondered why people didn't want to be my friend. I dressed in black from head to toe with heavy make-up suitable for a night club. I wondered why the preppies were not inviting me to their coffee klatches. I also worked full time at a restaurant driving on a motorcycle. None of this was working.

I had a deep moment of clarity after a particularly cruel night of drinking on an empty stomach. Life was never going to get better unless my behavior got better. I was the common denominator in all of my woes.

I was not a victim as I had been thinking. There are many details to this story, but the important part was that I stopped drinking that next morning. Forever. I identified a behavior that I needed to have the courage to change. To give myself time to heal, I deferred my college attendance until I got myself together. I went back years later and graduated Magna Cum Lade. Realizing that (and what) I needed to accept, change and surrender, changed my life.

You've heard the term, "self-sabotage" before. If you think back, what comes to mind for you? Without judgment, write the ways in which you do or once did this. If you have more than one, number them in order of importance to transform.

In order to shift your behaviors and thoughts you have to first know what they are. Then you decide that spiritually, energetically, mentally, and physically, you are going to let go of what no longer serves you. Bring this into your prayer and meditation. You are not in charge of when or how quickly the changes come. Only that you are open and willing.

*A*ffirmation:
"I let release all negative thoughts and behaviors."

Day 51

It is your Divine Right to live an Extraordinary Life.

Three things for which I am grateful...

1. _____
2. _____
3. _____

There is a beautiful yoga studio in my little town. One day, my teacher read a quote:

"I lovingly release myself and others from past hurts. I am free, and they are free to live an extraordinary life."

It hit me right in the heart. It was so simple, yet so profound. It's your Divine Right to live an extraordinary life and you are the only one standing in your way. Which means that suffering from past hurts, either received or given, is optional. You are not obligated to suffer another moment.

My life has been a series of interesting lessons. I feel as if I have had three lives in this one body. And all of my lives prepared me for the big spiritual leap. Depending on where you are in your life, you may relate. In the meantime, you and I get to live in the most extraordinary level of awareness and consciousness available to us today.

My entire mission is about informing and inspiring people through my work to live their most alive lives. For you to know your true value and worth in this world and to live in that knowledge. From that place of true freedom and worthiness, the answers for the questions you have will unfold.

Is there anyone, including you, that you need to forgive for past hurts? Use the mantra above to do that now.

_____

_____

_____

_____

Describe what living an extraordinary life looks like. What are you doing?

_____

_____

_____

_____

_____

_____

_____

_____

_____

_____

Who is participating in your adventures?

_____

_____

_____

_____

How do you feel?

Write it in the present tense, as if it is happening now.

Make a note of what tools you intend to use to realign to the present moment (breath, meditation, journaling, chanting, dancing, exercise, moving mediation, aromatherapy) so that you live an extraordinary life.

Affirmation:
"My life is happening in the now."

Day 52

You are a *Magical Being of the Universe.*

Three things for which I am grateful...

1. _____

2. _____

3. _____

The truth is that you really are a Magical Being of the Universe. You simply need to uncover the magic that is already within you. Wallowing in mistakes, imperfections, and forgetting your Divine Nature, are all in the past. Remember who you really are and how all the little human being moments are just that, moments in time. You will no longer hold them against yourself like some belittling scoreboard.

You are a "Magical Being of the Universe." Snort. The first time I heard that, I thought, "If only." Self loathing is an insidious thing. It's a useless practice perpetuating the big lie. I believed the lie for a very long time as I had no evidence to the contrary. The lies from my childhood included, "Life is hard. You can't trust your reality because it can change in a heartbeat without your input or permission. As a female you are less than. You are unworthy of a normal life. Watch out for the unexpected detour because it is always going to come. Don't be too happy because the other shoe will drop."

Some of these beliefs were unspoken by another, some were actually said. What this generated was a fearful, angry, mistrustful and yet entitled, young woman. Not a magical being. I was always suspicious and on guard. This could have continued to be my reality, but I opened my consciousness to possibility. I had to face my life not as a victim of the beliefs listed above but as a belief buster. My old reality was not going to be the end of my story. It took me years of searching and healing and receiving loving moments and experiences along the way to arrive at the truth: I am the creator of my reality through my thoughts and I get to choose what I think. What do I choose to think now? That, "I am a Magical Being of the Universe."

What are the negative beliefs that linger?

_____

_____

_____

_____

_____

_____

_____

_____

Flip the script. What do you choose to believe instead?

_____

_____

_____

_____

_____

_____

_____

_____

_____

_____

_____

Can you release your past beliefs with love today? What do you think?

_____

_____

_____

_____

_____

_____

_____

_____

_____

_____

_____

_____

_____

_____

_____

_____

_____

Close your eyes and Imagine accepting yourself completely. See yourself as a spiritual being with a human form. It is simply a journey of returning to the One.

*A*ffirmation:
"I completely accept and embody my divine nature."

Day 53

If the people in your life do not hold you up to the light,
They are no longer welcome to share the journey.
Release them with love.

Three things for which I am grateful...

1. _____
2. _____
3. _____

You deserve kindness and love. As Maya Angelou famously said, "When someone shows you who they are, believe them the first time." Don't make excuses for others. If they don't hold you up to the light of your highest good, let them go. Watch how you treat your friends and family. Do you break them down to feel better about yourself? Or do you hold them up to the light? If it's not kind, true or helpful. Don't say it. The energy of love is returned tenfold.

I once walked up to a woman I considered a friend. We had been to her house many times. Shared holiday meals, a neighborhood, and schools for our children. Our husbands were best friends for twenty years. She was in conversation with a teacher at the school and as I approached, she put her hand out like a crossing guard and said in a stern voice, "I'm having a conversation," and turned back to the teacher. I had planned on standing off to the side for her to become available. Yet, what happened instead, was invaluable to me. I realized that I had a poor definition of who I called friend. That was on me. I was also very sensitive and had not learned that it was not personal. Regardless, it was at a turning point in my understanding. A light bulb went on in my head. Why had I thought she was my friend? It wasn't because she was kind, listened to me, sought my company, or added to my life in any way. It was because I was a convenient prop to make her look good to others on her terms. Fascinating. Why in the world was I staying in a relationship with unkind or even mean people? I had no discernment. I had no programming that helped me choose who gets to participate in my life. I learned that you don't have to accept crumbs from other people and then try to turn them into a banquet. I did this with so many people and situations. Accepting what people were willing to give, not what I wanted or deserved. It was a pivotal moment and a lifelong gift that she inadvertently gave me that day. I am grateful to her.

Who are your friends? List them.

Next to each one answer these questions: Are you equals in your spiritual journey or are you seeking approval? Are they kind? Are you kind to them? Is there an exchange of life force energy or is there a vacuum?

If seeking approval, when you actually get it, do you feel better about yourself? Fulfilled? Do you feel relieved? Does it feel like a "fix"? Does it last or is it a bottomless pit needing another fix? Is it actually in their power to make you feel anything at all?

When you truly believe from the inside out that you are worthy, simply by being born and uniquely you, that inner foundation of love and acceptance will be your guidepost for how you feel about yourself. You no longer need to seek outside validation. You will inherently have unerring discernment.

Affirmation:
"I love, accept, and understand who I am and I am enough."

Day 54

Building the foundation is essential. If it is strong, your experience of life will be unshakable.

Three things for which I am grateful...

1. _____
2. _____
3. _____

My friend tells the story about a building that was once the tallest in the world called the Taipei 101. Just like life, Taipei is hit with a myriad of strong earthquakes and typhoons every year, so the foundation had to be solid. They spent years on planning and constructing the solid concrete foundation. The remaining floors were built in under a year. When you meditate, eat well, let go of negativity, challenge and fine tune your beliefs, you build that foundation of solid self-worth and a sense of who you are. This becomes unshakable in the turbulence of today's world.

How you do this will vary according to your personality. The anthropologist and leadership expert, Phillip Folsum, has studied wolves to understand various personality styles. He says there are four basic categories. The first category is the Warrior who is motivated by results and control. They are decisive and fast moving. The second is the Sovereign who is motivated by participation, praise and encouragement. They are fast and spontaneous. The third category is the Lover who is motivated by acceptance and security. They are slower and more relaxed. The last category is the Magician who is motivated by accuracy and precision. They are slower and systematic. I happen to be in the sovereign category so I move quickly and spontaneously and can change direction on a dime. There is no right style. They are all valid and necessary for the healthy functioning of society. Know yourself and build your foundation accordingly.

Think about the areas of your life you want to bolster. In career, it might be taking a course online or getting a certification in something about which you are passionate. That takes time and money, but it is an investment for the rest of your life. In relationships, maybe it's dating first, really getting to know another person and laying a foundation of friendship before becoming intimate or monogamous. This will serve you throughout the relationship and creates a better chance of sustained connection. In health, it could be implementing excellent nutrition for a foundation of wellness and strong immunity. In your spiritual journey, identify your foundation of values and adopt practices that set you up to win. This could be breathwork, journaling, meditation, and qigong or yoga to help prepare and guide you to the next level. Take time to connect with what matters to you and lay the foundation for a well lived and powerful life.

Today I will strengthen my foundation in each of these categories, career, health, relationships, finances, spirituality, hobbies, creativity, travel, family by...

_____

_____

_____

_____

_____

_____

_____

_____

_____

_____

_____

_____

_____

_____

_____

_____

_____

_____

_____

_____

*A*ffirmation:
"I am strong and I believe in myself."

𝕯ay 55

If nothing changes today, then nothing will change tomorrow. Resistance to change is the playmate of fear.

Three things for which I am grateful...

1. _____
2. _____
3. _____

If you have spent time with an older person, you will notice that their relationship to change can become more rigid over time and their perspective narrows. How they see the world is primarily from their past experiences and lenses. However, the people who embrace change, are curious about life, and question their own beliefs and habits, are the ones whose energy appears to defy aging.

My older daughter once asked me, "Mama, do you think people can change?" Based on my life to that point and my experience of my family of origin, I unwisely said, "No. I think at their core, people remain the same." I wish I could take that back and say, "Absolutely! I believe in people and their commitment to growth!" I'm not sure if she wondered about me, my mother or herself being able to change but my answer wasn't very comforting to her. I think back on my life, the people I have coached, my current partner and his life story and know to my core that you can change. The steps necessary for change are:

1. awakening to the need to change
2. the desire to change
3. the decision to change
4. taking action to change

Remember, according to the laws of the universe, change is the one constant and therefore, the inevitable truth of all life on earth. None of us escape change, so start a relationship of trust and empowerment with it now.

How do you feel when you encounter change?

Do you resist, get angry, push back, or get excited about the challenge?

Does fear kick in? What are you afraid of with change?

Given that change is inescapable, how will you now embrace the opportunity to/of change?

What do you desire to change in your life right now? Notice the feeling as you write about it.

What action toward your change can you take immediately?

*A*ffirmation:
"I gleefully embrace change."

Day 56

Embrace your feelings. They will not kill you.

Three things for which I am grateful...

1. _____
2. _____
3. _____

You must learn the art of changing your "state of being" to create lasting change. Could your happiness be as simple as that? Could experiencing joy be that easy? Yes, for most of us it's simply a matter of choosing to use healthier methods to shift how we are feeling about any given aspect of our lives. Use tools like music, walking, dance, or meditation to shift yourself and your state of being instead of something that is a temporary fix. Embrace your feelings, don't fight them or they will stealthily and steadily store themselves in your somatic body anyway.

I was overweight, unhappy and unhealthy. I was also stressed, overworked and hopeless. There really didn't appear to be a light at the end of the tunnel. For whatever reason, I finally listened to the little voice inside saying, "Why don't you go for a walk? Get out in the sunshine, listen to those Tony Robbins tapes? What have you got to lose?" So I did, and I was listening to one of his series when he said, the reason people overeat is to change how they are feeling. Duh. Pretty obvious. The problem is that when a person uses unhealthy behaviors to fix something, they have two things to feel bad about instead of one. It makes sense that I used food, because the first drug of choice anyone has access to is food. I was desperate to stop feeling bored, scared, sad, angry, or unworthy. Doritos, cookies, and ice cream literally stuffed the feelings down. But because of the added weight, I got to add remorseful and self-loathing to the list of negative feelings.

I had to learn to recognize and process the feelings before true healing could happen. As an adult, there are many other ways to take yourself out of feeling. Name any addiction. This applies to whatever "drug of choice" you use to block feeling. Scrolling mindlessly through social media, drugs, cigs, booze, gambling, Netflix, or sex. They are all ways of escaping the present and suppressing your feelings. So, find a way to cut out, or scale back on the unhealthy behaviors. Go to rehab if that fits your situation. Do whatever it takes to live well and free.

The most powerful thing you can do to process and heal these behaviors is to practice mindfulness instead. Become conscious, aware and mindful of what feelings are coming up. Where did they come from? What are they about? Where are they in your body? You can journal, get up and dance. Go outside. Walk in nature. Hug a tree. Up your vibration and you will not need the unhealthy habit to feel better. Clear the field for the feeling of fun. You can choose what you have always chosen and get what you've always gotten, or you can wake up and choose differently. If today was in fact your last day, would you waste a moment of time doing things that brought you anything less than joy?

How do you process feelings?

How do you numb them?

How do you avoid them?

_____

_____

_____

_____

_____

_____

_____

_____

_____

_____

_____

If you can, notice if there is a certain time of day, a witching hour, when it is the hardest to cope. What can you do to support yourself, especially at this time? If you usually have 3 glasses of wine at 5:00 and you're trying not to, maybe schedule an exercise class at that time. Or a regular call with your BFF until the urge passes. If you snack at 3:00 like you did as a kid, find a replacement behavior.

_____

_____

*A*ffirmation:
"I naturally and easily embrace feeling."

𝔇ay 57

The energy of who you are, affects and influences everyone you have ever met or will ever meet. Through the end of time and beyond.

Three things for which I am grateful...

1. _____
2. _____
3. _____

Remember the stone tossed into the pond which ripples and radiates out? That is you. You make a difference every single day with things big and small. A smile to a cashier. A kindness to a homeless person. A donation of time or money to those less fortunate. Political activism. Cleaning trash from your beach or forest. Cooking a meal for someone. A hug. Taking time to really "see" your partner or child. A wonderful side effect of your kindness is that the energy you put into the universe will come back to you, many, many times over.

For a myriad of reasons, I spent my whole life trying not to shine too brightly around the people in my life. It started with my mom. I didn't know I was doing it but it was a behavior I took into adulthood. With my marriage, I thought I was being the proverbial Woman Behind the Throne. Truthfully, I was hiding, dimming my light, not using my gifts. Again, he didn't ask me to do that. He encouraged me to do things that were my own, but it was safer to ride his coattails. I even put my girls on their own little thrones in my mind and raised them to shine and make a difference. But not me. Too risky. I was afraid I might fail, but even more so, I was afraid I might succeed!

Blessedly, I woke up to the truth. That I am enough, I make a difference, it's my divine right to live an extraordinary life and I left the old thinking in the dust.

It's your right too. To live an extraordinary life. Ripple out by being authentically you.

How will you ripple out today?

_____

_____

_____

_____

What is the stand you will take in your life?

_____

_____

_____

_____

_____

Living in "Generosity of Spirit" automatically manifests joy. Starting with you, make an intention to be generous and kind with your words and deeds. Then think about the people in your life. How will you show them a generosity of spirit today?

Affirmation:
"I make a profound difference in the world simply by being me."

Day 58

Making a mistake does not make you a mistake.
It makes you human.

Three things for which I am grateful...

1. _____

2. _____

3. _____

No one with a human brain bypasses the quirky element of remembering, re-thinking and overthinking. A cow in the pasture does not freak out over and over again about the passing of methane gas into the atmosphere. They don't think, "I hope no one heard that fart." Or, "That was loud, what will the other bovines think of me?" Your challenge today is to be more cow-like. Who cares what others think? Stop torturing yourself with things from the past that no one but you will remember or think about.

This overthinking is simply combat between your mind and your intuition. Your mind is formidable and is there to present information and map out possibilities for your intuition to process and decide on. Stop letting your mind beat you up with a memory long past. If you experience a speedbump, let the brain gather the information but then ask your intuition what is true? Is this a mistake or am I a mistake? Hint: You are never a mistake.

After I left home at 17, I got a job at a convenience store to make a living. It was kind of fun to play grown up at first, but the truth was that I wasn't a very good employee. One night, my friend and I got pulled over for driving stupid. The cops were pretty cute, so we flirted with them and though it wasn't the goal, they let us off with a warning.

In that conversation, I mentioned where I worked. A few days later, I was restocking the candy shelf and I heard, "Hey." I looked up and there stood Police Officer McHottie. I almost choked because I had just stolen a candy bar and stuffed the whole thing in my mouth. I couldn't even respond without spitting chocolate on his shiny shoes. I was mortified and ashamed. Not because he caught me red handed and I thought there was a Kit Kat jail cell in my future, but because I was ashamed to be eating candy at all. It tied into my already well-developed body shame. Funny thing was that at that point, I was a healthy weight. It was because I was out of integrity on all kinds of levels and it had been witnessed. It put him in an awkward position, so he pretended not to notice and waited for me to swallow the contraband. After he left the store, I never saw him again. But the shame stayed with me. It was a moment in time that came back over and over and over again to torture me and further whittle away at my self-esteem. I wish I knew about cow farts back then. I made a mistake. That's all.

For the following writing assignment, remember that a mistake is just a blip. It's just a thing that happened and everyone makes them. It is no longer a shame-fest or an opportunity to make yourself endlessly wrong. Everyone makes them. It does not make you a mistake.

What is a mistake from childhood that continues to haunt you and that you are willing to let go of today?

What is a mistake from last year over which you are willing to stop making yourself wrong?

What is a recent mistake that you can neutralize in your energetic field today by laughing at it? I mean it. Laugh at it. It changes your state and reduces or neutralizes the charge on it.

Describe how letting go of the impulse to revisit your mistakes raises your vibration?

*A*ffirmation:
"I release the energy around my mistakes."

Day 59

You have the capacity to look into another's eyes and truly see them. To give to them by witnessing them. Acknowledging their existence in this way is a precious gift.

Three things for which I am grateful...

1. _____
2. _____
3. _____

Bearing witness to another's presence means we see and acknowledge them. I believe it also means that we hold space for that person. To be. Not just their physical body but their energetic and spiritual bodies as well. This inherently means we honor their journey unconditionally. Learning to do this for yourself will also assist you in witnessing others.

I met a woman when I was eighteen. Her name is Shannon and we have the exact same birthday. Same day, month and year. We bonded over this, and the fact we were lying about our age to work at a restaurant that served alcohol. We became the best of friends. She had two things that I did not: a handsome fiance and a dad. I found this endlessly fascinating. What must it be like to have that feeling of being loved and protected? So, I was drawn to her and her family. When she and her now husband moved to LA, I decided to transfer to UCLA. I stayed at their very cool vintage apartment for a couple of months while I got on my feet. She told me her husband said, "Joni's a nice girl but she never looks me in the eye when she talks." I didn't realize I did this. I didn't feel worthy of being seen or heard. It freaked me out. But I decided to work on both my self-esteem and my eye contact. There is a vulnerability in truly seeing people. The eyes are the windows to the soul, and I was afraid that if they truly saw me, they would run for the hills in terror. When I learned to be present and truly see, I tapped into a new charisma and people wanted to be around me.

Later, the practice became not only about holding my own space as a person but making others feel significant too. I don't have to imagine what that must feel like for that person. I now know.

Exercise

Today's exercise is more about how you "see" you.

Go to the mirror. Look into the eyes of that precious being before you and really see you. For some of you, this will be a piece of cake, for others, it may be devastatingly difficult.

There is no right or wrong here. Just notice.

Write down the feelings that came up.

Can you begin to let go of those judgements (lies)?

Maybe you felt love and acceptance? Write it all down.

Do this as many days as you feel inspired and notice how much easier it becomes.

𝒜ffirmation:
"I witness myself unconditionally."

𝔇ay 60

In the end, it's who you are in the
time you have, that matters most.
Not what you've acquired.
Not what you've done.
But who you are.

Three things for which I am grateful...

1. _____
2. _____
3. _____

There are three distinct phases humans traverse in a lifetime. In each of those eras, you have opportunities to completely reinvent yourself. To integrate and learn from your previous journey and go to the next level of transformation and evolution.

The first phase is "Who am I?" This phase is particularly intense through the twenties. I had so much childhood programming to unpack and unwind that I probably didn't have a clue who I was until I hit my thirtieth birthday. It's a tumultuous age of discovery. If you are here, breathe dear one. You will survive and thrive.

The second phase is "I know who I am, and this is what I'm going to do with it". This is the foundation building and acquiring phase. The striving for success and for some - status. For me it was marriage, children, and playing the game of the American Dream. It meant, "keeping up with the Joneses". Buying a house, two cars, and having a couple of children. Now, it's "Keeping up with the Kardashians" which is a whole other chapter we won't go into. Regardless, comparison is a brutal trap. So is the trap of, "As soon as I get this or that, I will be happy."

If you are in this middle phase, let go of caring what anyone thinks or has. Let go of needing things or status to prove your worth. Enjoy the time you have and yes, make money, be successful but PLEASE be present and spend time with people who matter in situations that inspire and fulfill you.

The third phase is "Who am I now and what is my legacy?" It's common for people in this phase, usually their fifties, to return to a more esoteric or spiritual place in their lives. They begin to look at what really matters to them. They see the difference or impact that they have made, or want to make, and shift focus to furthering that journey. For me I wondered, "How can I be the best me and use it to help as many people as I can in the time I have left?" If you are in the third phase, it is never too late to be who you came here to be.

My third phase probably started a little early. I began to wonder, "Is this it? Am I someone my children can be proud of? What difference have I made? How will I be remembered?" I didn't like the answers that came back, so I went back to school. I got an Executive Leadership coaching certification, a second bachelor's degree in Metaphysical Counseling, and a Yin Yoga certification from Bali. I voraciously read books from Wayne Dyer, Don Miguel Ruiz, Abraham Hicks, Brene Brown, Gay Hendricks and the Harvard Business Review on Emotional Intelligence, Spiritual Psychology and more. I studied or did DBT (Dialectical Behavioral Therapy), EFT (Emotional Freedom Technique, AKA Tapping), EMDR (Eye Movement Desensitization and Reprocessing) and EIEIO. I did everything I could to learn, be a better person and feel truly alive. I wanted to achieve maximum results in the quickest time possible. I knew I needed to change and I wanted to change fast so that I could hurry up and enjoy it. But transformation takes the time that it takes.

Remember, it's never too late to change. Sometimes you just have to trust and believe that you are on the right path. No matter what third you are in, you are exactly where you need to be. Everything that has happened has brought you here.

Are there things you want to shift or change now? What are they?

How will you go about this?

You are never too young to answer the question: What is the legacy you want to leave behind in the end?

How do you want to be remembered?

_____

_____

_____

_____

_____

_____

_____

_____

_____

Imagine you are on your deathbed. How will you answer this question:

Looking back, I know my life mattered because...

_____

_____

_____

_____

_____

_____

_____

Affirmation:
"I am becoming."

Day 61

It's never, ever too late
to be who you are meant to be.

Three things for which I am grateful...

1. _____
2. _____
3. _____

The human body carries the Soul or rather, the Soul co-operates with the body, so that you can live, connect, love and experience the miracle of life through the human senses. That's the whole enchilada. "You are a spiritual being that has come here to have a human experience" makes perfect sense. That means that your Soul is perfect because it's part of the One. Your human brain and body are beautifully flawed so that you can experience and learn as you go. If you honor your mind and body as your teachers, rather than fight them, you can embrace the lessons with curiosity and gratitude.

I used to bludgeon myself daily. On a daily basis, I put myself under a microscope and judged myself as lacking. From my aging body, to my flawed parenting, to my limping marriage, I blamed myself for it all. What I learned was that each of the players in my life had their own spiritual lessons to learn and I was not in charge of their reality. That meant each person in my nuclear family had their own exploration for which they incarnated. To think I was in charge or responsible for their mistakes, their judgements, their self-sabotage, their challenges and for that matter, their happiness and life victories was fallacy. It was utter ego to think their mistakes and pain were my fault or that their brilliance was my doing. We are spiritual beings who have chosen families, roles and identities in this lifetime for our expansion. The understanding is that we are all part of the One and therefore not separate. When my egoic self wants to take credit for any of it, I need to laugh and tell it to sit down. Honoring that each person has their own journey and it's really not my business to be their cruise director. It's my business to align with my Highest Self and live in joy. If they want to enjoy the ride with me, then so be it!

To be who you are meant to be, means to surrender, accept and honor your journey. It also means to honor the journeys of those in your life as perfect for them, no matter what it looks like.

How will you honor your journey and that of your human vehicle today in each of the following?

Mentally:

_____

_____

_____

_____

_____

_____

Physically:

_____

_____

_____

_____

_____

_____

Spiritually:

_____

_____

_____

_____

_____

_____

_____

_____

Energetically:

_____

_____

_____

_____

_____

_____

_____

_____

_____

Affirmation:
"My body is a divine temple."

Day 62

The twist is that you did not come here to be loved.
Or to collect the most toys. Or to win.
You came here to love.

Three things for which I am grateful...

1. _____

2. _____

3. _____

When you seek to get love outside yourself, disappointment may come in various forms. When you show up to love others, with no expectation, the very experience of "being love" creates the energy of love within. It's self-generated and available at all times. There is no neediness because there is nothing to "get." Only the giving of love and through that, self-acceptance.

I sought to fill the black hole in my gut with outside sources -- food, alcohol, relationships, and various experiences for many years. There was literally not enough of anything to fill the "God-sized" hole.

Most of us were taught that you need to get stuff to win, feel complete and be happy and fill the hole. You were told to be better, faster, better looking and more successful than others to feel satisfied or complete. I believed this and the target for me wasn't even wholeness, it was to feel less fractured and empty. Did you know that the word "sin" has been mostly hijacked as religious but it is also an archery term that means to "miss the mark." I was missing the mark completely by trying to fill my spiritual emptiness with things, places, experiences and people. When I woke up and made the connection that all of my woes stemmed from my lack of connection with my spiritual self, my inner divinity, I could do something about it. I was able to consistently connect through learning, meditation and prayer to heal. The longing went away because I was creating self-acceptance, connection and love. I was truly able to be here to love.

Do you see how the old way of being is to seek love and other outside things to make you happy? Describe how you once did this and what you do now.

Why is the goal of loving others, rather than seeking love from others, more satisfying and sustainable?

Affirmation:
"I am here to love."

Day 63

The human "suit" is a remarkable thing.
It allows us to experience existence in
the physical form here on planet earth.
The pleasures of eating, hugging, drinking,
physical activity and orgasm require a body.
It's your friend. The care and feed of it matters.
So love it well.

Three things for which I am grateful...

1. _____
2. _____
3. _____

Let's return to this subject as it is an important one. We are told through social media, magazines and billion-dollar industries of diet and fashion, that we are never enough as we are. We are never thin enough, our butts aren't big enough or they are too big. We are not young enough, smooth enough, fashionable enough, tall enough, short enough, light enough, or rich enough to be happy. We must spend money and seek the newest fad or fob to find happiness. This has been going on for centuries with the standard of beauty shifting and changing over time. It's all about money and money is about power and influence. They tell us at every turn that we are not enough. So we need their products to change into their "ideal" to feel worthy. Did you know that the powers that be sold tapeworms to women last century so that they would lose weight? Then the consumer would have to take a cure to kill the tapeworms and of course they would gain the weight back and the cycle continued. Money made on both ends. They have sold us pills, shots, HCG, colonics, diets, fat farms and many more money makers all the while saying that we need to pay for this and suffer this way to be accepted and loved. The funny thing is that the standard of beauty keeps changing so the source of unhappiness is never ending.

I have dealt with body image and weight issues my whole life. I learned it from the above as well as witnessing the suffering of my mother and older sister. Both stunningly gorgeous. Both obsessed with being too fat. They weren't. Up and down and all around they went. Addicted to weighing themselves and weight loss. I was confused but I adopted the trend once I hit 15. Lost forty pounds in two months starving myself with cabbage soup. Gained it back the minute I started eating food because the obsession kicked in and a bag of cookies a day with an ice cream chaser seemed like a good idea.

I found myself trapped in a quagmire of, "as soon as." I would love myself as soon as I was thin. I hated myself if I felt I was fat. Fat meant I was unlovable. So as soon as I was thin, I would have a relationship, wear cute clothes, I would be happy. How much time was spent wishing to be somewhere else, looking like someone else? I can't get that time back, but I can be gentle, loving and accepting with myself that I did my best. My amends to my younger self is to treat me with dignity and respect.

It's time now to look at your relationship to your personal Divine Temple - your miraculous body. What do you think and feel about it? What do you say to yourself about it? Are you willing to let go of punishing or judging your body on any level? I said are you WILLING? If the answer is yes, then begin here.

Describe the attributes of your body for which you are grateful. I know you have them.

_____

_____

_____

_____

_____

_____

_____

_____

_____

_____

_____

Now write to your body thanking it for its resiliency, strength, health, and power.

_____

_____

_____

_____

_____

_____

_____

_____

_____

_____

Let yourself sink into loving acceptance and listen for the intuition you have for what needs to happen next to help you heal and live in freedom with yourself.

Close your eyes, breathe twice through the nose and one long breath out the mouth. Do this twice. Now pray this prayer, "Great Spirit, I thank you for the honor of this body. Please return all of my body's cells to Source (God's) Perfection. Help me love, accept and nurture my Divine body. Thank you." Do this daily and feel your body blossom.

Affirmation:
"I am healthy, self-loving and strong."

Day 64

You can create a strategy or a plan all you want.
But if you don't change your thinking,
you'll get the results you've always gotten.

Three things for which I am grateful...

1. _____
2. _____
3. _____

They say, "Progress, not perfection." It's about creating forward momentum and not judging setbacks. The trick is to live life with grace, not black and white perfectionism.

For years I watched my mom (and judged her) while she would buy a new sales kit which she was certain would make buckets of money. Back in the day, and maybe still, the marketing strategy was to get "housewives" to buy these multi-level marketing sample kits and they would then sell the products to the public and become rich. She bought Mary Kay, protein powders, Herbalife, clothing lines, jewelry kits, healthy snack lines, etc., and never sold a thing. She wore the fake sample jewelry and polyester clothes, drank the protein shakes and consumed the weight loss bars. She was going to write a book, get a face lift and be Oprah. There was always a scheme, a plan or a pipe dream. She was an intelligent, beautiful and powerful woman in her own right, but she didn't know how to really know that. Instead she was flitting from place to place looking for the "fix". The cure. The scheme that would finally make her feel successful and whole. Bless her heart.

I see all of this now and her legacy is that her pain and experience taught me that nothing from without can fill us within. It also taught me that if we always do what we've always done, we will always get what we've always gotten. She never stopped to change her process to get a different result.

If only she knew how valuable she was.

She is no longer with us so of course she knows quite a lot now. I learned from her that committing to something and following through is critical. That life needs to be lived from, and for our purpose. That everyone makes a difference. That humor is a critical tool for elevating our vibration. That negativity, self-doubt and judgment are cancers that infect us and keep us small. I also learnt that I don't have to be Oprah to be of value. "O" is a brilliant channel of change and transformation that has inspired and affected probably hundreds of millions of people. But there is only one unique her and one unique you. You too affect the people in your life in a million ways. The Universe doesn't care about your achievements, it cares about your heart.

Set yourself up to win with a plan. This plan is not an outside-in quick fix plan. It is an inside job so create a plan for new and healthy habits that will contribute to a forward momentum in your life. It needs to be specific and doable for you.

What else do you commit to accomplishing today? Be specific. Why are you doing it? When will you do it? Where will you do it? What is it that is going to be done?

In the evening, review your day. How does it feel to keep your word with yourself?

Tomorrow: Rinse and repeat. Before you know it, you have massive movement in your life.

Affirmation:
"I follow gleefully follow through."

𝕯ay 65

Be deliberate.
Deliberately choose the puzzle pieces of your life.
To create the most beautiful and best version of you.

Three things for which I am grateful...

1. _____
2. _____
3. _____

Extraordinary does not mean grab a cape and save Gotham City.
It means to be so present, so often that all of life, including you, is
experienced fully. Go beyond what is usual, regular or expected
and create your own brand of magic.

If you watch a leaf floating down a river, it can only travel at the
speed of the current. It is buffeted, turned, dunked and directed.
This is the way of things. If the leaf is you in your life's stream and
you surrender to its process, you will be content. But if you think
you should go faster, turn left or right but have no intention or
plan in place, you may be unhappy.

If you just float along from birth to death with no intention, you
will eventually get to your destination. If the leaf had an intention,
it might be to enjoy the journey of floating downstream. Or if it
had eyes, to observe the river with curiosity and learn from it. If
you're constantly rushing and struggling to get somewhere, you'll
miss all the beauty you can see along the way. Your life journey
lived with deliberate, conscious choices will make it
extraordinary. That means setting intentions and being present
for the peaks and valleys along the way.

Now back to the leaf. Before you jump in the stream, look, choose your path and your destination. Then make a plan. Pick up a couple of little oars. Do not fight the current. Figure out the path of least resistance to your goal. Stop on a rock to rest. Hitch a ride on a log. Watch the blue sky go by. Grab onto a branch. Sunbathe on the shore. There are so many ways to live your life. The key is to live YOUR life, not to let your life circumstance, history or others dictate how you live.

You know what it looks like to just let a day happen to you. You wake up. Work. Eat. Sleep. Rinse. Repeat.

Describe the same day and week unfolding but with the lead actor, you, being fully present, curious and imaginative in the interpretation of the people and events.

_____

_____

_____

_____

_____

_____

_____

_____

_____

What would you do differently?

_____

_____

What would you deliberately pay attention to?

_____

_____

How does it feel to go to the coffee shop today? The beach? The gym?

What are the sights and sounds of being totally present?

Affirmation:
"I am fully present and transcend the ordinary."

Day 66

"Wherever you go, there you are."
You cannot outrun your shadow.

Three things for which I am grateful...

1. _____

2. _____

3. _____

Nothing improves or changes significantly simply because you change your hair, move to a new city, transfer to a different school, get a new job, or change lovers. So stay present and do the work. Change the insides, and your outer life will follow. It's less scary and more efficient to face yourself and have a functioning life than to try and run from yourself forever. You can do this!

I once took a hostage—I mean had a boyfriend. He was a nice guy and I was super young and really had no clue how to be in a relationship. But he had been married and divorced and was ten years older and I thought maybe my being raised by wolves would not get in the way. It was clear that we wanted different things and in fact we were not a good match, but I stayed in the relationship for a year just to prove to myself that I wasn't broken. That I could have a relationship. When I knew that it was over, rather than be honest and lovingly explain that it wasn't going to work, I announced that I was transferring to UCLA. I was "pulling a geographic" by changing locations to fix my life. No discussion. No truth. I thought he'd be sad but let me go, no problem. Instead, he said, "I'll come too. We can get a place together." He didn't want to know that I was running from him. And I didn't understand that I was running from me. I'm not proud of this moment but it does highlight what our best thinking can look like when we do not have the tools for healthy living.

I eventually told him that I didn't think it would work. My ego thought it broke his heart but of course, I don't have that power. He met a woman, married and had a family not long after that. I went on to create drama and make more poor choices and continue to run from myself. However, no matter how many times I tried it, wherever I went, there I was. I really thought (hoped) that it must be circumstances of my life making me unhappy. Then I could fix it. But I came to know that I had to address my shadow side. To heal the fractures. To take a stand and stop running from my self-perpetuated unhappiness as if it was a thing I could outrun.

Where are you running in your life?

What does "running" look like for you?

How will you take a stand for change?

_____
_____
_____
_____
_____
_____
_____
_____
_____
_____
_____
_____
_____
_____
_____
_____
_____
_____
_____
_____
_____

> # *A*ffirmation:
> "I face and embrace myself."

Day 67

The tunnel may be the shortest route to where you're going
but it will not be the most scenic.
It's about the journey, not how fast you can get to the destination.

Three things for which I am grateful...

1. _____

2. _____

3. _____

Life is not about taking short cuts. It's about enjoying the journey.
The sights, the sounds, the smells, the people, the experiences. In
the end, it is our experience of life, ourselves in relationship to
others and Spirit that matters.

My life has been like Angel's Landing in Zion National Park.
Trudging through switchback after switchback, squeezing through
a rockface, and then tip-toeing down a narrow rock pathway just
to reach an absurd landing. It was worth every step, walking
through every fear, standing at the end feeling like Wonder
Woman. My first attempt was with my favorite, and only, cousin
Lisa. She is a study in perseverance and courage. But that's her
story to tell. We hiked Zion together and after talking and taking
pictures and observing the valley below, we came upon the
beginning of the end. It is a vertical climb up a section that leads
to the narrow single person paths edged by a chain. People have
actually died on this hike and I was no spring chicken but after
my Grand Canyon hike, I was game. We talked about it and she
said that with her knees, she wanted to sit the last segment out,
but she would wait for me. So, I decided to try it. It was the
perfect metaphor for life. I was moving through the fear, knowing
that I was as prepared as I needed to be, and the Universe had my
back. But I also realized once I started that the wind was pretty

strong and while I was surrounded by other hikers, I was alone. So, I paused. I thought what am I trying to prove? I can be a beast another time when the prospect of me plunging to my death was less likely. A little dramatic but my truth. I knew that I could probably do it but having never been, I opted to go back and live to try another day.

That day came several years later with my new partner. He'd been before. In fact, he'd been hiking and sporting his whole life. So, when we did our Zion, Brice, Moab tour, it was the perfect opportunity to revisit the possibility. I was more fit, I was carrying less weight. I was completely ready. It was exhilarating. Brilliant. Breathtaking. Empowering. But to be honest, the first time was just as empowering because I did my best and though it was a different choice, it was my measured choice. It was not from "I can't", but from "I choose not to, today". Sharing the journey with people I cared about made all of it sweeter. Life on life's terms means that we show up and we do our best in every situation. We face the switchbacks of life head on and we don't judge, knowing that our best will vary from day to day.

Where do you think you should already be in life? What do you think you should already have? Should you be richer? Thinner? Smarter? More educated? More followers? Famous? Happier? Is the grass always looking greener somewhere else?

Now write about how perfect the journey of your life actually is for you. What are you learning along the way?

𝒜ffirmation:
"I am exactly where I am meant to be right now."

Day 68

Hold the space for others to have their own experience. They may not be done feeling pain. They may not be ready to wake up. While it may make you uncomfortable or sad, honor what's necessary in this moment for their evolution.

Three things for which I am grateful...

1. _____
2. _____
3. _____

Letting go of others takes non-judgment and non-attachment. Be the love you would wish for yourself. This will help you avoid taking on their process or feelings. And it will allow room for them to grow. The only person you can change is you, and the only life you can live is yours. This allows others to be exactly where they need to be too.

My friend of twenty years, whom I love and adore kept repeating experiences in her life that were causing her pain. She kept pointing out how mean people were to her. How they were all trying to take advantage of her. She kept talking about how cheap people were and then nickel and dimed everyone. Yet, by the standards of 90% of the people on the planet, she was very wealthy. I'm sure the scarcity mentality came from a deeply ingrained past wound, to which I could certainly empathize and relate.

When she asked my opinion, I tried to help her understand that she was not a victim and she had a choice and to see how she was setting herself up over and over again. The cycle continued. I started to get frustrated. I wanted so badly for her to get it and to set herself free. Why couldn't she see it? That she was the common denominator and she was the one imprisoning her heart with her beliefs and then her anger that there was not ever enough. Part of me wanted to hasten her awakening so that I would feel better. But even if I laid out the truth in detail, which I did, a person must be ready to hear it. One day I said to my partner, "Why can't she let go of her suffering?" He said to me, "Not everyone will wake up in this lifetime and it needs to be alright with you, or you will cause your own suffering."

With whom in your life do you need to stop over involving? This does not mean to cut them off. It means who do you need to hold with gentler hands?

What boundaries do you need to set for yourself so that you don't overstep your role? For example, only give advice if asked, stop checking up on them, don't judge.

What fears will you have to let go of in order to allow them their own journey. Remember, fear is behind every urge to control or change another person.

Visualize your new relationship dynamic. How does it look and feel?

_____

_____

_____

_____

_____

_____

_____

_____

_____

_____

_____

_____

_____

_____

_____

_____

_____

_____

_____

_____

_____

_____

*A*ffirmation:
"I fully live my own life."

𝕯ay 69

Challenges and conflicts are not the enemy.
Conflicts can even be healthy debates,
Not wars with emotional hostages & blitzkriegs.
Challenges are simply opportunities to learn more about yourself and life.

Three things for which I am grateful...

1. _____
2. _____
3. _____

If you come from a background of volatility, conflict may be a way of life in your psyche. It might feel dangerous and triggering, yet strangely familiar. If you come from a loving background, conflict (not violence) may signal an exciting opportunity to learn more. To find common ground and grow. Most people fall somewhere in between.

For me, feedback, conflict and challenge were a personal attack. I thought that having conflict meant the person or situation was rejecting me. It probably comes down to the limbic system and our fight, flight, freeze or fawn reactions. For me, I would freeze. Like a human doll with big eyes blankly staring and hoping the danger would pass. For good measure, my second reaction was to cry. My unhealthy coping mechanisms were meant to help me survive the moment. And that may have been true and necessary as a child, but now they just got in the way. I worked with a man when I first started doing workshops. He had zero approval stuff and he could smell other's neediness for acceptance and approval from a thousand yards. I knew it was my opportunity to finally neutralize this old pattern. One day he demanded the blinds be shut because the sunlight was making the room too hot. I said I'm already on it and he said something like "Are you?" And I said, "Dude it's not rocket science, I've got this." In other words, stop micromanaging, I said it's handled. Rather than pick at me, he laughed. And I realized that stuffing my words, my feelings only made me a bigger target. But that pushing back with the same energy of power, in a respectful way, worked way better.

If you need a moment in a stressful situation or are triggered by conflict, the most powerful thing I was taught was to pause and ask questions. Like, "Hmmm, that's interesting, can you tell me a little more before I respond?" Or "Can you give me an example so that I can fully understand before responding?" That gives your brain time to come back online and the prefrontal cortex to engage.

Until you realize that nothing is personal and it's just information that can help you know how you are being perceived or where you need to put your attention, you may try and avoid these things. What if you stopped resisting them and welcomed the opportunity to learn and become more conscious and adept at life? With challenge, you can change or fine tune your approach.

Do you avoid conflict, or do you run toward it, even manufacture it? Why?

_____

_____

_____

_____

Do you stuff your feelings to keep the peace? Is it working for you?

_____

_____

_____

_____

What are key phrases you can use that diffuse the tension and allow people to stay present and work through the conflict?
"I really want to understand your side of things, can you tell me more?"
"It feels like we are headed for a blow up, maybe we can sit down and talk about it in about 30 minutes from a calmer place?"

You can create an agreement ahead of time that you are both going to try to communicate better in a future conflict. That creates an opening for either of you to de-escalate the energy so that you can both be heard.

Do you see where you may have room to improve, as Brené Brown puts it, your "Rumbling" skills? It begins with personal accountability and an open mind. If you need to be right to feel safe or seen, you're in trouble.

Shift the need to be right to the need to understand. In order to get there, you will need to heal your relationship to conflict.

*A*ffirmation:
"I trust myself to stay present and have my own back in conflict."

𝔇ay 70

Approach life as a mystery. A puzzle to solve. Relax, it takes as long as it takes.

Three things for which I am grateful...

1. _____
2. _____
3. _____

You have a right to ask questions and explore your life at your pace. Another of the Four Agreements by Don Miguel Ruiz, is "Don't Make Assumptions." If you are assuming things, you are making things up about events or what you think is in other people's heads. To avoid this, learn to get curious and ask questions.

I am not sure where I learned the false assumption that I was supposed to know everything already. And if I didn't, I acted as if I did. That's exhausting. It also meant I missed out on a lot of things. I have dubbed my partner Curious George. He asks questions about EVERYTHING. At first, it felt weird and intrusive because I asked nothing. Then I thought I would give it a try. I began to say things like "Interesting, tell me more? What makes you think that? Thoughts?" If you are in a mode of discovery instead of thinking you know, your brain is far more open to possibilities and wonder.

Curiosity is actually genius. The opposite, the closed mind, is so boring. As the human being ages, without concerted effort to stay open, their perspective narrows. You have seen old people with twinkly eyes and a zest and joy for life. Those lovely creatures do not think they know. They still approach life with a childlike (not childish) wonder. Knowing that they do not have to know and that's a very good thing. The fun is in the discovery.

Since curiosity is the playground for the open mind, how are you willing to live in that space today?

What specific situations or people do you plan to approach with wonder? How?

Affirmation:
"I live in childlike joy and wonder."

Day 71

As people, we will be solving the mystery of life
for as long as we are living.
Your job is to simply live in curiosity and enjoy the ride.

Three things for which I am grateful...

1. _____
2. _____
3. _____

The point of this journey is to continue to expand. The journey, like the human being, is imperfect. So, judging it as flawed is a waste of your time. Get excited that you actually got to come here to planet earth and play.

As a young child of five years old, I wanted to know who and where God is and how He came to exist. At seven, I wanted to know, if this Being was so "all loving", why did people suffer? I asked my parents at nine, why people were treated differently because of their skin color, that it was wrong and unjust and by the way, were Angels real? At thirteen, after a long conversation with a dooms-dayer, I wanted to know if Armageddon was true and imminent and, if so, should I even bother going to college?

Things shifted when I reached twenty-five and my brain began to make better sense of the world around me. I learned for the first time that it's infinitely fulfilling to be of service to others. At thirty-two, giving birth made me feel like anything is possible. By forty-one, the song "Is that all there is?" was looping in my head. I felt like I was digressing. Going backwards. I began to realize that happiness and understanding are like the waves of the ocean hitting the shore. They come in and go out as your awareness changes.

Life is not a straight line, so I had to stop fighting the zig zags. The overarching truth that has guided the journey is that we are spiritual beings that have come here to love. As such, the goal is simply to remember who we are. To uncover your core truth one layer at a time. How one gets there is unique to each of you.

Write a mini story of your life here.

Can you identify some of the most important questions that you had? They don't have to be positive or negative, just impactful on your trajectory. Did they get answered? What are you most curious about now? What is behind the curiosity? What do you hope to feel from knowing the answers? Can you adopt a perspective of curiosity without a need to get anything right?

Affirmation:
"I make a difference simply by being me."

𝔇ay 72

Figure out a solution then make a plan.
Surrender the results.
They are perfect for this moment in time.
Then move on. No drama.

Three things for which I am grateful...

1. _____
2. _____
3. _____

When we don't hang our happiness on the results of a thing but instead see the value of the journey, we don't live in expectation of an outcome. We'll all encounter challenges, problems, and puzzles for which we may need to find a solution. This means we take action, we surrender the results to the universe and we accept and respond to the outcome. This is the opposite of trying to control everything which is exhausting and counterproductive.

Drama was my middle name. I stayed married for three years before I was brave enough to agree to get pregnant and have our first child. I kept thinking we had to have all our financial ducks in a row before I could surrender to bringing a new life into the world. The truth was that I wanted to control the ducks so that I felt safe. I wanted to make sure my husband and I were going to make it as I didn't want to divorce and be a single mother. I wanted to have a home for the children to grow up in. I also wanted four babies... until I had one. I was dumbfounded how anyone could do it. We agreed to move forward, didn't figure out a very good plan or solution to the finances and house but we did surrender that there would always be something to work on. A wayward duck. It was my second huge surrender to life's path and trusting that all would work out. The first was the day I got married.

I did have one last request (control) of the Universe regarding children. Please send me boys. Not girls. Boys. Because I was raised by a single mother with two sisters and a female dog. I knew how difficult it was to deal with the complexities of the female human and I wanted an easier ride. I would deal with the boys jumping out of trees and the emergency room visits and the smelly socks. I didn't want to deal with highly emotional and hormonal girls like me. I later realized it had a great deal to do with my inability to hold the space for my own wild woman. I was born to parents from another era where the dads were disappointed if they didn't get their desired sons. Ridiculous, I know. I wanted boys, not because I considered them better, but because I was tacitly taught that as a girl, I was less. I didn't want that for my girls and frankly, I was terrified to go through what my mother had to endure. Teenagers are really powerful in their chaos. God laughed and gave me two girls. Not any two girls, no, two girls who had I.Q.s so high they were outsmarting their mother by the time they were eight.

Don't hear me bragging about their intelligence, it's literally just an aside. My ego-self used to brag to anyone who would listen, but then I realized that 1), I didn't actually make their brains, and 2), they were smarter than me, and 3) I had to parent that.

Here's what happened when I realized I was going to have a girl. I said fine, if that's how it was going to be, I'm going to learn how to love myself as a female and to champion them as females too. It did help that giving birth naturally and under water planted the phrase deeply in my psyche, "I am woman, hear me roar." I made a vow that I would never tell them they couldn't do something because they were girls. That they would have the same right to power and their voice as anyone else. I saw how not getting my way was in fact, for my Highest Good.

I was right that it would be complex and even painful to be a parent, but it was so worth it. That is the long way of saying that nearly every time in my life that I think I know what is best, I have learned to say, "This or something better." Becoming a mother made me a better woman and eventually, a better person.

The lessons, deep love and many adventures were better than I could have imagined or planned. Being a mother is the most powerful role I have ever played and it's only getting better, richer and deeper with time.

I want that for you. That you can say that you have learned to make a plan, let go of the results and let go of drama in your life because you have the tools to make that choice.

Think of a problem in your life that you would like to solve. What is it?

Why does it need solving?

Pray and meditate for 10 minutes. Ask for the solution to become apparent.

What solution came to you?

Outline a plan based on that solution.

_____

_____

_____

_____

_____

_____

_____

_____

Execute the plan with the prayer, "This or something better, I surrender the results." How does this approach feel to you? Is it uncomfortable? A relief?

_____

_____

_____

_____

_____

_____

Affirmation:
"I let go of the expectations in my life and live in the process."

Day 73

Don't settle for the life others may try to spoon out for you. Get your own spoon, make it a big ass scooper, and have at it.

Three things for which I am grateful...

1. _____
2. _____
3. _____

Think back to your parents and their parents. Have you noticed that they have beliefs, often inherited, such as, "I will make sure my kids get a proper upbringing and education, shield them from the bullies, bubble wrap them and keep them safe until they go off to the college that I choose for them, and get the relationship I want for them...so that I feel better." Most parents simply want to do what they think is right for their child, not realizing how fear based their need to orchestrate to the nth degree really is.

What if instead, every parent said, "I love you. This is your journey. You will make the mistakes you need to make. I am here for you. There is nothing you could possibly do to make me love you any less, or anymore."

This story is about my younger daughter who has never settled or done things because other people said she should. She had a difficult time connecting to institutional education. She had three different high schools as we tried to find the right fit. I knew she was hella-smart but she just hated the whole system. Being bullied didn't help. I said to her, "Please just graduate and let me get a photo of us in your cap and gown." Then I will be happy. I was actually afraid that not having a diploma would limit her choices. I was also afraid that her not getting a diploma would make me look like a bad parent. Though getting there was a trek, she stuck it out and graduated. Afterwards, I continued to try and control things "for her own good," and asked her if she would be willing to go to a community college to see if anything inspired her? I even flew us to Hawaii to see if she might be enticed to go to college there. I thought I could bribe her with paradise! Remember, she's a smart cookie and my well-intentioned manipulations didn't work. Standing in her own truth, she beautifully found her own path.

In truth, I was operating out of my own beliefs and experiences about what it meant to succeed and be happy. Luckily, she was operating out of curiosity and faith that she would find what would inspire her. She said to me with maturity and clarity, "Look, I want you to know that I will probably never go to college." Over time she said, "I want to take classes in yoga, reiki, cranial sacral therapy, meditation, breathwork and yoga nidra. Can you please help me talk to dad?" I had surrendered by this time and said, "Absolutely." His wise response was "Whatever makes you happy". Even though his background was deeply rooted in the value of higher education, he knew she was a free spirit.

We honored that she needed to find her own purpose in her own way and in her own time. Had we insisted that she fit into our box, "or else", she would have said "or else." That would have forever changed our relationships. Though a gentle soul, she is also a powerhouse and was meant to walk a completely different, unique and inspired road that has rippled out and touched many lives. She did not settle for the spooning out of life that her parents thought was best. She didn't settle for what society was spooning out either. Forget the spoon, she picked up a shovel and went to town on her own path.

Whether you are a parent, have a parent, or know a parent, most importantly and empowering, <u>you are now your own parent</u>.

Take a moment to breathe and center yourself. Imagine you are a vulnerable and innocent age.

What do you want that young you to know?

How will you honor and protect her/him? Start with "Dear (insert your name),"

Now, if you are a parent, write the same loving letter to your child. They could be 5 or 35. It doesn't matter as the healing comes when it comes. From a place of trust and love. They may never read the letter but let them know how you will do better.

✠Affirmation:
"I will do my best to parent myself from trust and unconditional love."

𝕯ay 74

You're the master of your destiny.
It's time to reinvent yourself again,
to align with that destiny.

Three things for which I am grateful...

1. _____
2. _____
3. _____

Being the master of your own destiny means that you are
empowered to choose how you live and experience the journey.
Maybe your destiny is predetermined, maybe it's not, but how
you get to the end of the story is up to you. One of the hardest
things you may ever learn is to choose you. Not from a self-
centered place of me, me, me, more about me. It's about how do I
take care of myself emotionally, physically and spiritually so that
I can be fully present for the people in my life and my journey? If
you choose to reinvent yourself, do it for your Highest Good and
the Highest Good of others. You will find the thoughts and actions
of self-care and unconditional love (for self and others) come
more naturally. From this place you will not give up your dreams
and your aspirations by living through (or for) others. Live for
you. Hiding your light sucks. No one asked you to do that. Or
maybe they did. No one who is conscious wants you to do that. In
fact, it is essential that you shine. Be the example, the beacon.

I purposefully chose to be a stay at home mother. I was a latchkey
kid and didn't want that for our kids. But in the process of that, I
found that I was hiding from my fear of failure AND my fear of
success. If I stayed at home and created "Camp Joni" playdates
and constructed LEGO fantasies and sheet tents with my kids,
gave life to their stuffed animals, microwaved chicken nuggets

and picked up dog poop all day, then I didn't have to dream my own dreams. I had the excuse that I was doing something noble. I was curating future leaders of the world. Plus it was so much fun, to be honest. The truth on a deeper level was twofold. I was avoiding the historical and ancestral healing that needed to happen by filling my day with little people. Plus, if I never tried to create a business or career, then I couldn't fail.

Fast forward post marriage and empty nest. I came to a crossroads. It was now or never if I was going to own my voice and make a difference in the way I knew I could. I looked at the long and winding road ahead and asked myself this question, "How do I want to live my last thirty years?" I chose to reinvent myself and align with my destiny. I educated myself. I revamped my health. I reshuffled the time clock. I basically reverse-aged by becoming playful, curious, adventurous and joyful. We don't know how many days, years or hours we have left. There is that proverbial "You could get hit by a bus tomorrow" adage. So how do you want to live it today?

Definition of Destiny: "something to which a person is destined; a predetermined course of events"

My destiny appears to be...

How I will align with my destiny today is...

How I can reinvent myself just for today is...

As the master of the experience of my life, I choose to feel the following...

You become the master of your destiny when you choose to feel these things now. Imagine and visualize the feeling you will have when you achieve mastery. Actually, see the expression on your face. Feel the happiness well up inside of you.

*A*ffirmation:
"I am now living in alignment with my destiny."

Day 75

Let go of what no longer serves you
and make room for the beauty and abundance
waiting for you.

Three things for which I am grateful...

1. _____
2. _____
3. _____

What no longer serves you is different for everyone. They are usually habitual thoughts based in old beliefs.

What no longer serves me is playing a small game. Is pretending that I am less deserving or powerful than the next person. This mental game of comparison goes way back for me. I remember asking my fiancé. "Am I bigger than that girl in the crosswalk?" This is a no-win situation for your partner and instead of answering the question directly, he said, "Why do you do that to yourself? You will always find someone thinner or prettier or richer than you if you are comparing yourself to others. You can't win this game and it's not fair of you to involve me in it." I was nonplussed. I knew at that moment that he was perfectly right, and it was a no-win habit I had learned.

I was also angry because I wanted him to hop aboard my unhealthy behavior. Misery loves company and he wouldn't buy into my small game. So, I vowed to let go of it because it wasn't serving whatever warped need I thought it was filling. Of course, I felt infinitely better. I was to let go of many of those over the years. As they would become apparent, I would write about them and ask the Universe to take them. Sometimes it happened right away, other times, it would be months later, and I would realize that I had been set free of it.

Think about it. What behavior or thought pattern, or limiting belief can you let go of today?

Possible behaviors: Eating on automatic. Not meditating. Over committing. Negative self-talk. Gossip.

Possible thoughts: "I'll never make a million dollars. If I was thin, then I would be lovable (or happy), what makes me think I deserve XY or Z? The world is a scary place."

Possible Limiting Beliefs: "I've never reached a goal in my life and never will, people like me never get ahead, I need an education or higher degree to be successful, life is hard, money doesn't grow on trees, my kids don't appreciate me, I need a significant other relationship in my life to be happy, people are against me."

Now, I want you to challenge yourself. Is the thought, belief or thought pattern actually true? What purpose does it serve? Or was it simply inherited and woven into your own behavior over the years? Hint: It's never true in the present.

Most importantly, what is the positive replacement thought, belief or behavior you will begin right now? How will you reinforce it daily?

---

*A*ffirmation:
"I release all negative thought forms, beliefs and imprints that no longer serve me."

𝔇ay 76

Don't hide who you are...the world needs you.

Three things for which I am grateful...

1. _____
2. _____
3. _____

There is no other you. There is an old movie called, "It's a Wonderful Life" starring Jimmy Stewart. It is a classic black and white feel good Christmas movie. If you haven't seen it, find it and watch it. The point of the movie is that without you, every person you have ever known would be affected and that you matter deeply. There is something called the "Butterfly Effect" developed by a scientist and meteorologist which is a theory that even the flapping of the wings of a butterfly halfway across the world could influence a tornado. That somehow the disturbing of the air around something as small and innocuous as a butterfly could change things in a noticeable and perhaps profound way. You are that butterfly. You are important, valuable and necessary to the fabric of the here and now.

As some of you may know, I have been doing a podcast since December 2018. There isn't a lot of real time feedback in doing a podcast and it is work to get the guests, do the homework, edit the podcasts, etc., and I never monetized it. I was doing it because I really, truly wanted people to be able to have the information and tools to live their best lives. But I also did it because I was afraid to do it and I wanted to push myself. Then I ran out of steam in 2021. I thought I would just take a break and wait for the inspiration to begin again. What difference was it really making, anyway? Then I moved to a small town. There I met a woman, a healer. We struck up a friendship and many conversations. I had sent her one of the podcasts that was germane to one of those talks. Next thing I knew, she was consuming them voraciously. Podcast after podcast and she would tell me every time she saw me, what it was that struck her or made a difference. I could see and feel in real time how the information she was absorbing was transforming her life. I was inspired by her and vowed to reboot, reinvent and relaunch the podcast. My butterfly wings were rippling out in ways I had no idea and cannot quantify. I was blessed by this beautiful feedback but it doesn't matter anymore. I will continue to post Youtube videos and podcasts and next, maybe even Tik Toks videos in trust that someone, somewhere will receive what they need. Always remember, you are uniquely you and fully worthy to be here.

The most extraordinary butterfly gift you can give the world is to be authentic. To be you.

How will you know that you are aligned with your true self? It's all in how you feel. There is a peace, a joy, a groundedness to being in balance and centered with your True Self.

Write about how you are unique and worthy. How your smile, your artistic gifts, your scientific mind, your humor changes the world of the ones you love and ripples out into the world. Notice if this is hard or easy for you. This is not about ego, this is about the humble truth. You matter. Set a timer and don't stop for at least 10 minutes.

Affirmation:
"I am deeply unique and worthy."

𝔇ay 77

Connect to your inner quietude.
It is where the wisdom and voice of your Higher Self resides.
You will be amazed at the Divine information waiting for you.

Three things for which I am grateful...

1. _____

2. _____

3. _____

No other species on the planet deals with the concept of unworthiness the way human beings do. All of us at some point have a version or form of it. Unworthiness is a collective illusion and a lie yet everyone has experienced it. The only voice you should be giving credence or credit to is the voice of unconditional love within. That's the True Voice and you can receive guidance, peace and love from there.

I spent years tap dancing as fast as I could so that people wouldn't notice that I didn't belong here. Not just belong to my family, or my community or my school, but to the world. To humankind. I really tried to appear capable and cool. To say and do all the right things. To avoid discomfort or rejection. But that means I was always playing life on the defense. A great sports team has both a powerful defense and offense. We need to have that too.

Be proactive in what you want to create in your life in terms of relationships and abundance. Don't wait for life to happen to you. Make it happen for you. Going back to the sports team, a good offense is critical but without a solid defense, the game is going to be a fight to gain any ground and keep it. In life, your defense for what life throws at you is the ability to be agile emotionally. To be able to not take things personally, be resilient and curious as well as communicate effectively. To do all of that, you must be authentically you. Not a made-up version you think is going to get you what you want. In order to consistently do that, you will need to go quiet and tap into the real you.

Meditation is the best, most powerful vehicle for connecting to the inner silence and vast information that I have ever found. "How do I do that?" is the question I get literally every week. Answer: A little at a time.

Meditation Prompt

You may have been avoiding that scary place of "being" for years. There is no "right" way to do it. The only wrong way is to never try. Earlier you used a touch stone to help you focus. Today, continue to expand your mediation practice in whatever way works for you. You can focus on your relaxed breathing. Don't try to empty your mind or stop thinking, just notice the sounds in the room, the texture of the chair or bed, the thoughts that ticker tape across your mind. When they come, just go back to what is happening now. That's the key.

Expand your meditation practice to a minimum of twenty minutes a day. You can do more but for noticeable results, do it consistently. Meditation is key to aligning your inner and outer world and it is the pathway to the quantum field of possibilities. It is a way of accessing the subconscious as well as connecting to information available beyond your form.

Affirmation:
"I easily and effortlessly meditate every day.

Day 78

Since the shadow side exists for us all, to deny it will not serve.
So, when your "dark side" presents itself,
don't swallow it, judge it or deny it.
See it, feel it and heal it.
Set yourself free in degrees.

Three things for which I am grateful...

1. _____
2. _____
3. _____

What is the shadow side exactly? Carl Jung said that the shadow functions are the unconscious parts of our personality. Not as sinister as you might first think. The shadow elements usually show up when we are anxious, stressed or having a hard time coping. It's the part of ourselves we do not normally admire. The part who projects, blames, judges, is irrational or uncivilized. Don't fight it. What we resist, persists. Instead, thank the shadow for being the catalyst for change and growth. It shows you the contrast of who you do, and do not, want to be. Acknowledge that while those characteristics have served a purpose, you are now ready to let them go.

Years ago, my daughter Allie called me. I was driving at a snail's pace in rush hour traffic and welcomed the company. She started telling me in detail about her experience with a healer who explained to her that she had a "shadow side". I began to get uncomfortable. I was thinking if this kid has a shadow side, I must have a shadow sphere. I listened as she explained about her dark side. The parts of us that can feel ugly and even frightening. I asked her to explain more about what she meant by the shadow. She said that if she, or anyone, is going to heal, the shadow must be embraced. It's part of our unconscious mind and if ignored, it can actually cause significant issues and even illness. With absolute innocence and clarity, she went on. In order to be whole, both halves must be acknowledged. If we do not, we begin to live fractured lives by looking at and embracing certain parts of self while ignoring or subjugating the ones you don't like or aren't pretty. It will bar you from your true self-love. As she spoke, my shame spiral started to kick in. I had been walking around with my shadow hanging out my whole life. I should have known, I thought. I should have healed it before I had kids, not found out about it from my adult child. I teared up and started to apologize. I wanted to beat my chest and throw myself at her mercy. But she would have none of it. She said, "Ma, stop, it's ok, we all have it and we all have ancestral stuff and honestly, we've all done the best we could, Including you. And I love you and I am so grateful for you." So, I say to you dear reader, welcome to the knowledge of the dark side. It's good news because you can now set yourself free in ways you never dreamt.

How does your shadow side appear?
CLUE: Think of the parts of you, you least admire or want to push down.

Looking at your answer to the first question. Where did the characteristic or behavior begin? Are you now willing to let it go?

Ask in your prayer and meditation for your higher power to remove those elements. It may happen miraculously and it may take time but in time, you will be able to look back and clearly see the shifts.

*A*ffirmation:
"I am now ready to lovingly surrender the parts of me that no longer serve my highest good."

Day 79

Do what you love and you open up worlds.

Three things for which I am grateful...

1. _____
2. _____
3. _____

You have heard the phrase, "Follow Your Bliss" which means do and be what brings you joy. If you are aligned with your purpose and your values, you will be aligned with your most powerful self. From that place, all things are possible, and joy is the norm. Abundance can come to those in their Bliss because the vibration is higher and will attract more positive events and experiences.

From the time I was a little girl, I wanted to be a doctor. Actually, at five years old, I asked my mom for a doctor costume for Halloween. She bought me a nurse's outfit instead. Don't get me wrong, I now see nurses as the backbone and heart of our medical system, but back then, it was a not so subtle sexist message that even as a child I recognized. I still wanted to be a doctor all through high school but around the time I graduated, I realized that there were a lot of moving pieces to applying to college. I had no idea how to navigate the system and had nothing in place. So, I decided to do the next best thing and skip college to wait tables. I realize now, this would later play into my parenting. Waitressing was easy cash which was my escape from a volatile homelife. After a few years, I decided I wasn't really cut out for it.

I wanted to help people as a doctor, but more importantly, I wanted the prestige and self-esteem that came with the role. That identity...so that I would feel worthy. I was one of those very smart kids in a small pond, or should I say fish bowl.

I started at the local UCI and then transferred up to UCLA where I was no longer one of the smartest kids. I was one of 40,000 really smart young adults. They strangely seemed to know how to navigate life. We always think everyone else knows what they're doing but mostly they are faking it until they make it too. Or maybe they had a solid family foundation. South campus was for pre-med students. I quickly realized that I would have to work hard and study. A lot. So instead, I decided I would become a lawyer. Not because I loved the law or wanted to fight for justice, but because I would feel powerful and make a lot of money. It was still about the need to feel worthy. Then I decided that law was way too much work and I hated conflict so I thought, "I know!" To get the love and attention I crave, I will become an actress." Yup. No segue. Nothing in between. Doctor to attorney to actress. Truth be told, I was very good at it, but I was such a mess as a person, that I had zero confidence. I knew I didn't have the fortitude to be rejected once, let alone over and over again at auditions.

What did all three career choices have in common? None of them were driven by a higher purpose to serve. All of them were about money, fame, accolades, prestige, people pleasing and acceptance. Not about passion or drive. All of them required hard work, commitment and dedication which I did not have because my why, my reason for wanting them, was faulty.

This brings me back to "Do what you love, and you open up worlds." The happiest, most content people are not the ones who make the most money or have the most prestigious jobs, they are the ones who are doing what they believe in. What they love. You can be a pig farmer and be very passionate and in love with the process and the land. You can be a cowboy or own a quilt store and be in love with the process and the happiness it brings others. You can be a tech billionaire and be in love with how you have the ability to change the world.

How do you want to serve humanity? That's the question. What I do now is that. Through my writing, podcasts, Youtube videos, coaching and showing up as the most loving version of myself that I can each day with friends, family and strangers. That is how I serve. I can't wait to wake up in the morning. Every single day. It was not always that way because I thought that the things outside myself were going to bring me worth. Until I realized that the only way to achieve that was shifting to being worthy just because and unconditionally loving others while following my bliss.

How have you tried to get self-worth from people, places or things outside yourself, including how you look, or speak?

What would you jump out of bed to begin doing or being each day?

Who are the people that inspire you? What do they have in common?

What brings you joy?

_____

_____

_____

_____

What matters to you?

_____

_____

_____

_____

What are your core values?

_____

_____

_____

_____

What is your mission?

_____

_____

Affirmation:
"I live my life with purpose."

Day 80

Show up fully, as if it is your last chance to love.

Three things for which I am grateful...

1. _____
2. _____
3. _____

Regardless of the number of years you have been here on planet earth, treat each day as if you will not have the chance to love another day. Don't wait to tell your parents, children, friends, lover, that they matter, and you appreciate and love them. Thank them for being a part of your life. Witness them by telling them what you appreciate about them and how they make a difference in your life. Don't be stingy with your love energy. You will be energetically rewarded 100 fold but that is not the reason for doing this. Do it because it is aligned with your truth.

Life can be a lot. Every decade you are alive brings new and sometimes mysterious, sometimes annoying, sometimes joyous phases of development. It can be confusing, exhausting or wondrous. There have been times in my life where I would question what was it all about? Was the pain worth it? Then always, I would arrive on the other side of whatever challenge had me questioning my existence. It took me a long time to arrive at "It is better to love, than be loved." I had it backward for a long time. There is a very old song by Peggy Lee and part of the refrain kept playing in my head in my 40s. It goes like this, "Is that all there is. Is that all there is. If that's all there is, my friends. Then let's keep dancing." I remember this well because I had thought that marrying well, having children, a golden retriever, four cats and eight guinea pigs, a house and two cars in the garage would make me happy. I kept looking out and forward for happiness. In fact, I was staging an illusion of normalcy based on what I thought society expected and accepted. So that I would be happy. I bought the old "American Dream" smoke and mirrors created by marketers. They wanted to sell houses and cars and told us that if you have this or that, you will be happy.

But having a family and being responsible for the care and feeding of other beings is fraught with pitfalls and challenges of its own. A family (relationships) is a living breathing organism which cannot be predicted. Remember, looking outside of yourself to others for your identity and validation will always end badly. By their very nature, relationships will morph and evolve and do not exist for your validation. They exist for you to love so show up fully. Even if they annoy you. Love as if it is your last chance.

Make a list of 2-5 people in your life that are your core inner circle. It can be family or friends (or both). Decide how and when you are going to contact them. If it's your grandparents, and they are distant, a card with a hand written note (include a photo of the two of you if possible) may be appropriate followed up by a call. They are from the snail mail generation and it is their communication currency.

If possible, wait until you are in front of your person. Or call or Facetime but no texting unless it's the only way to contact. You want to have the maximum love impact. When you get a hold of them, simply state your experience of them and how you love and appreciate them. All positive.

Write how it felt to give them that gift.

What did you experience with each of your people?

_____

_____

_____

_____

_____

_____

_____

_____

_____

_____

_____

_____

_____

_____

_____

_____

_____

_____

_____

_____

_____

Affirmation:
"I am vulnerable, courageous, and loving."

Day 81

You can play life to lose.
You can play life to "not lose."
Or you can play life full out to win.

Three things for which I am grateful...

1. _____
2. _____
3. _____

Playing life to win is playing with courage.
Playing life to lose is playing in defeat and fear.
Playing life not to lose is staying in the comfort zone.

This concept was taught to me by my mentor long ago. It was a light bulb moment for me as I realized the not so subtle difference in how we live our lives. I played mostly in the "not lose" category. I didn't make waves, didn't garner successes, and didn't question the lie or my life. I rarely felt unbridled joy and pretty much just got by on "having potential" and never stepping into my power. That way I couldn't lose. But the truth was that in not trying, I lost anyway.

The best illustration of this was right after I was married, my husband asked me now that we are married, "What would you like to do with your life, Mrs. Lerner?" I was working with him in his office and he knew that it probably wasn't my forever inspiration and I said, "I want to go back to college and finish my degree." He was very supportive, and I started the reactivation process at UCLA right away. Some time later, I received the acceptance letter and was almost paralyzed. He came home and asked, "Why are you staring at that wall?" I said, "I'm afraid to go back." Even though I loved the process of learning. He said,

"Why?"

"Because I never win at anything." He said, "How long have you been sober?" and I told him "Five years". He said, "I'd call that a huge win." Woah. Wow. And a double take. He had hit the nail on the head. In that scenario where my very life was on the line, I was playing to win. I could do this! I could play with courage. It was a pivotal moment in my life where I shifted from the unconscious belief that I was a loser - so I didn't want to play in case everyone else found out. To the conscious choice that it's better to have played the game and take the lumps or the wins, than to stand on the sidelines in a mediocre life.

Take a moment to imagine the three scenarios. Playing to win, not to lose and to lose.

In work, in relationships, with family and with friends, which of these do you use?

_____

_____

_____

_____

Are you willing to play life to win in at least one area (or all) today?

_____

_____

_____

_____

_____

_____

_____

How will that look? What will be different?

Affirmation:
"I play to win."

Day 82

Make snow angels wherever you can.

Three things for which I am grateful...

1. _____
2. _____
3. _____

The act of leaping into a mountain of fresh snow may not be available to everyone, however, it is a fun metaphor for life. To leap with joy and abandon. To giggle and not care who's watching. To feel the exhilaration of novelty and child-like wonder. That's the goal.

I spent much of my life worried about what other people thought. Trying to play by the rules and color within the lines all so that I would be accepted by others. I am not sure where I learned the original lie that if others approved of me, then I would feel accepted, legit and therefore safe. As you have been on this journey with me, you have heard through a series of learnings, that I made a choice to live my life, not what others expected of me. In that process I discovered a child-like being within.

I decided to go big or go home. For several years, all I could do was get my girls ready for school in the morning and see them out the door. In my undiagnosed but obvious depression, I would then close the curtains and go back to bed until it was time for them to come home. I was eating comfort foods in bulk, drinking diet coke as if that would offset the calories, and not moving my body at all added the one hundred pounds to my body. I had become a shell of my former self. No one, not even me, recognized me and I had to stop and take a stand in my life. I just didn't know where to begin.

I chose to begin to do things that scared me and forced me to come alive again. I started by buying leggings that fit and going to the gym. I committed to twice a week and even if I ate horribly the day before, I had to go. It was my commitment and agreement with myself. I added music concerts to my life because my kid wanted to go, and she was only fourteen and I felt better if I was there and on hand. We went to several annual Coachella's to be exact. I began to add more things that were scary and out of my comfort zone. Day by day, I felt more alive. I was still huge, but I was participating in my own existence instead of passively letting life happen around me.

I went hiking. Not in my backyard. In the Grand Canyon. I bought a new pair of hiking boots which I had never owned in my life. I read up on how to hike. Seems pretty simple but if I was going to hike the Grand Canyon to the Supai village and Mooney Falls, I needed to prepare. No one could have prepared me for the adventure that unfolded. After hiking eight miles the first day, I had to lie down on the bed with my legs up the wall so I could get blood back into them and hope to be able to move again. The next day the guide took us to a water fall and my wildly athletic friend said, "Let's jump! I thought, "Are you completely insane?" And instead, I said, "Yes!" Knowing the guide would say, "No!" He didn't, and I had to jump because I said I would. He had said that if you didn't jump at the right spot, you would hit the rocks. My friend said, "Here?" He said, "No." She moved and said, "Here?" and he said, "No." She moved again and said, "Here?" He said, "Yes!" And two seconds later she was gone. Which made it my turn. I had been paying attention, went to the spot from which she disappeared over the edge and said, "Here?" He said, "Yes." But I remained in place, white chubby knees bent and stared over the edge. I couldn't see my friend below the outcropping but I could hear here yell, "Come on! It's amazing!!!" I was muttering to myself, "The only way out of fear is through" and with the guide's gentle and kind words of encouragement, I leapt off. I hit the water and was so exhilarated that I was still alive that I kept repeating in my head, "I am woman, hear me roar." The adrenaline rush was profound. We didn't rest on our laurels as we then hiked down Mooney Falls.

At the top, the guide said, "We can turn back or we can hike down through the rock face with just a chain to help. It's a one-way system as there's not enough room for more than one person at a time." The other couple in our group declined but my friend and I were still so pumped, we let him know we were down to do it. He taught us the three-point system of keeping a combo of at least three touch points (feet and hands) in order not to fall to our death. Dramatic but true. That day, I realized that I could do just about anything I chose. That it was in fact, the choosing that mattered.

I traveled again and again, doing things that challenged me to expand my horizons. Not to the next state, or town. To other foreign lands. I ate authentic food and rode with Gauchos on the Pampas in Argentina. Flirted with a cute gaucho who I probably outweighed by 40 pounds but there is just something about a cowboy that makes you feel alive. I explored the Blue Mountains of Australia. I skipped on the black and white boardwalk of Rio De Janeiro in Brazil. I cried at the majesty of the love I felt surrounding the massive statue of Christ the Redeemer.
I kept going. Exploring the fairies of Galway. Did you know that they spent millions of dollars rerouting a highway around a fairy bush? They take their magic very seriously there. I continued on to a whirlwind double decker bus tour of Paris dancing through the Louvre and down the Champs De Lycee. Communed with the energy of Stonehenge and explored a castle in Edinburgh.

Finally, I literally learned how to ski and made snow angels in Big Sky, Montana. I went from feeling that my life's adventure was pretty much over to wandering this beautiful world with a childlike wonder. What I came to learn is that I didn't have to go anywhere to make a "snow angel". That simply being present in life regardless of where I stood, was the magic sauce to emotional freedom.

Your snow angel could be riding a roller coaster, sticking your head out the car window and fully feeling the wind on your face with music blaring. It could be trying a new sport, a new food, or calling a friend just for the joy of it. It could be giving yourself fully to the experience of connecting with another human being.

How will you make "snow angels" today?

---

*A*ffirmation:
"I live my life with joyful abandon."

𝕯ay 83

Surrender and acceptance
are the most powerful places to live.
It means that the ego,
which strives to keep you separate,
is not driving.

Three things for which I am grateful...

1. _____

2. _____

3. _____

Ego is a funny thing. The ego will likely hate the use of the word ego. It needs to survive in its role no matter what. Ego, or the little self, also serves a very important purpose. It lives in the middle of the conscious mind and will forever exist. It creates individuality as a person and therefore the knowledge that you, as an individual, not only exist but can make a difference. You will always know that the ego is driving the car when things are not feeling aligned. You may feel agitated or uncomfortable, judgy or less than.

On my spiritual journey, it was suggested by a 12 Step program, that I figure out my character defects and ask God to remove them. It's a very powerful practice because we often don't even realize that most (all) of the pain we suffer is of our own making. Even though I didn't think I had any defects of character, I was willing to look. What I discovered was mind blowing. I saw all the ways I used negative behaviors to protect myself and to give continued life to my ego. They also called the ego a defect of character. In this process I thought, "I totally get why letting go of being judgmental, self-righteous, gossipy, living in anxiety and low self-esteem would be beneficial, but ego? Who would I be without my ego? She has protected and defined me for so long, wouldn't I cease to exist?" I thought my ego was me. What I didn't realize was that the ego was not only my individuation as a person but when out of balance, the umbrella for all the other defects. It took me years to know that I could ask for the negative aspects of ego to be removed. Ego itself is not negative and is never completely removed because it is part of "me". It is the thing that tells me you are you and I am I. In balance, the ego is not driving the car. It is a passenger and a tool.

The process of living in surrender and acceptance means doing your very best from your Higher Self, not your ego or little self, and surrendering and accepting the results. It may not be what you think you want at that moment, but it will always be what you need.

Make a list of the habits, thoughts or character defects that are still causing you discomfort or pain. These are associated with the little self, or ego.

Once you have the list, read through it. Then ask Source to remove them. Some will go immediately. Some will take time.

Now make a list of the replacement thoughts or behaviors that are more aligned with your Highest Self. Write your intention to live from this place.

𝒜ffirmation:
"Today, I live in harmony with my ego but rely on my Higher Self."

Day 84

Let go of the stress of anxiety and worry.
In fact, let go of stress and anxiety.
You see, the Universe has always had your back.

Three things for which I am grateful...

1.
2.
3.

Anxiety is always caused by fretting about the future. It's about something that hasn't happened yet and very probably won't. Hours, days, weeks, years can be dedicated to projecting into a future that rarely ever manifests. It's wasted life energy spent on rumination. Think of all the energy and power you take back when you let go of stressing yourself out either with blame about the past or worry about the future.

The feeling of being anxious can be low grade and persistent or it can be situational or chronic. If you are prone to it at all, understanding that the common denominator in all anxiety is fear will help you release the need to engage in it. Think about what you worry about. It's usually fear that your needs are not going to be met. Or fear that something bad is going to happen to you or around you. The underlying fear is that you won't be able to handle the situation or event.

Throughout my life, I operated from the drive for security so that I could stop being afraid. It caused a great deal of anxiety for me. I can't begin to tell you the litany of things I feared. My dad once caught a giant potato bug and put it in a block of resin to preserve it. There it sat, day after day as his new paperweight. It was deeply ugly to my child's eyes, like a bulbous-headed alien, but it never changed. It didn't deteriorate. The bug didn't get its feelings hurt. It would literally last forever, frozen in time. If I could have done that to my children and then break it open when they were safely at 20, I might have. Not really, but the need to protect myself from hurt extended to them. If anything happened to them, I would cease to exist.

That same anxiety and fear of vulnerability kept me from truly falling in love for a long time. It drove my need to control the aspects of our family life. It kept me awake at night worrying about money. It permeated the fabric of my life and bled over into my daughters. If I would have known better, I would have done better. But having healed that cellular need to fret, I have set myself and others free and you can too.

List your top two or three worries that currently plague you.

For each of these, what is the fear?

Are you willing to see the fear is not real at this moment but is a trigger that causes you to try and control things?

_____

_____

Now shift from the fear of what <u>could</u> happen, to being in this moment, right now, and focus on what is true. Write it down. Notice how much positive energy is freed up when you stop focusing on the negative.

_____

_____

_____

How will you use the "NOW" on creation, innovation and joy?

_____

_____

_____

_____

_____

Affirmation:
"I live in the now of creation."

Day 85

To move out of the darkness,
You must be willing to courageously shine a light
 on the truth of your being.

Three things for which I am grateful...

1.
2.
3.

Let's delve into the concept of "the darkness" or the "shadow."
The darkness can be the feelings of sadness, negativity,
depression, scarcity, hopelessness and even simple frustration. It
can also be negative thoughts, beliefs and habits that keep you
from your highest level of joy. It could be the negative aspects of
your personality. What's true is that if you speak, feel and release
your feelings, they cannot fester. But if you run from the shadows
and live in denial, they will rule you. They will grow and live in
your somatic body and invisibly influence your life decisions and
experience. You cannot run. You cannot hide. The good news is
now you know that some of the unwanted events or experiences
in your life have been created or steered by the subconscious
shadow. Once you wake up to its existence, you can clear much of
it and manage the folly on the rest until that too is released.

I didn't really know this. I lived in a weird reality for many years. I
pretended that my mother's alcoholism and my older sister's drug
addiction and mental illness were not my problem. Once they got
into recovery and on their way, I believed I could just move on
and create the life I wanted. I didn't realize that addiction or
mental illness (or both) are not "their" problem. It is a family
problem. It affects everyone. I was carrying a burden not of my
own making. But of my own keeping.

Their struggles affected everyone. How my little sister and I viewed and navigated the world was colored by those dynamics. We interacted in a dysfunctional way in relationships as a direct result. I figured if I just moved on and created my own reality, I could begin fresh. I could orchestrate and move the pieces of my life and the people in it like a human chess board. But "Wherever you go, there you are." Not dealing with my shadows marginally worked for about 20 years. I say marginally because I was not living an authentic life fully in my power. I was denying the experiences that colored who I am. I thought I had hacked the system. My house of cards came crashing down once my older daughter hit puberty and the triggers of her struggle became a mind field for me. Everything I had not dealt with came roaring back as PTSD and rendered me largely ineffective as a parent. I was in permanent fight or flight for about a decade. If you add the years together, that is 30 years of carrying and living in the "trauma drama" that, like the fish in water who doesn't know it's in water, became my emotional fishbowl. I didn't know better. Until I did.

What negative feelings do you want to process and release today?

What would you say are your shadow thoughts, behaviors or habits?

What are opposite thoughts or behaviors you can adopt?

_____

_____

_____

_____

_____

_____

_____

_____

Without judgment, are you ready to let go of some of these and make peace with your shadows?

_____

_____

_____

_____

_____

After you have thoroughly examined your feelings, spend 5-10 minutes in meditation or quietude. Ask for what you are ready to release to be removed.

𝒜ffirmation:
"I am now willing to have all negative thoughts, imprints and beliefs removed. Thank you."

𝔇ay 86

Leave every person you meet better for having known you.

Three things for which I am grateful...

1. _____
2. _____
3. _____

There is a term, "generosity of spirit." If you are generous with your energy, your love and acceptance, you and the people you bless with it, blossom. If you live in resentment, that is you taking the poison and hoping the other person will die. If you live in anger, you are putting your health and happiness at risk. But if you live with a generous heart, all things come more easily and relationships and energy flow.

Imagine what it is to encounter a loving person. Now imagine what it is like to encounter an angry person. As a waitress, I devolved into a very resentful yet entitled young woman. When I first started waiting tables, I was grateful to be making enough money to live. As the years passed, my partying increased and I felt stuck, my attitude slipped big time. I knew it was time to quit and change careers when after being particularly snarky, I was left a pile of pennies for my tip. Even though I probably deserved less than those few cents, I was enraged. My unworthiness got triggered. I followed the people out into the parking lot and threw the pennies on the asphalt at their feet, and yelled, "You forgot something". As they tinkled down the incline, I turned on my heel with righteous indignation and left them standing there with shock on their faces. Of course, I couldn't look any of the patio customers in the face. They had just gotten a show and it wasn't pretty. I knew at that moment that I had crossed a line from quirky to bent. I needed to change how I was showing up to life or my behavior would only worsen. It would not be long before I lost more friends and probably my job. It took a while to find my generosity of spirit but find it I did. And once you fall in love with yourself and everyone else, you can never go back to playing the tiny game of negativity and resentment.

I am neither above or below my fellow human beings and everyone deserves to be treated with dignity and respect. From the clerk at the 99 cent store to the neurosurgeon to the spiritual master and everyone in between. Every time I do this, it adds to my self-respect. It makes me feel good and connected to the powerful energy of love that is there for all of us should we choose it.

Write down your intention today for being generous of spirit. Notice throughout the day, how you feel in this mode.

What do you notice in the reactions of the people in your life?

_____

_____

_____

_____

_____

_____

What about strangers? Are they surprised? Delighted? Confused? Remember, the legacy you leave is made up of not only the obvious, but of the thousands of tiny gifts that weave through the fabric of your life.

_____

_____

_____

_____

_____

_____

_____

_____

_____

_____

Affirmation:
"I create a generosity of spirit throughout the day."

Day 87

Self-love. Self-acceptance. Self-care.
Loving others.
These are the ingredients for happiness.

Three things for which I am grateful...

1. _____
2. _____
3. _____

If you have been taught that self-care is selfish, you must reassess. It is not selfish to take care of you because in that process, you become more. You become all that you are capable of and that energy, or love, can then be shared. Think of any superstar human that you admire and study their habits. I guarantee you that they have a discipline of self-care which includes variations of breathing, meditation, exercise, reading books and healthy eating. Self-care is a personal obligation to be fully charged so you can plug into possibility.

If you give and give and give and give and refuse to receive, paradoxically, you are a taker. You take from yourself and deplete your ability to enjoy and be present in your life. When Allie was somewhat younger, she said, "Mom, I can't, my cup's not full." She was saying that she didn't have the bandwidth, or energy stores, to handle one more thing that day. I'm sure it was some mundane topic that I was beating to death so that I felt better. I liked to plan ahead. But I respected that she didn't "people please", she told the truth and I dropped it.

When you feel you just can't have a conversation, or go to a party, or answer the phone one more time today, don't. If you think about that cup, if you keep pouring out your energy to people or things but you don't replenish it, the cup will soon be empty. That is how your energy works. Receiving is necessary.

You are encouraged to sleep well, meditate, journal, eat well, receive, read, dance, laugh and play. Each of these acts of self-regulation fills your energetic cup.

Make a plan for today, tomorrow and the rest of the week. How will you fill your cup?

Affirmation:
"I easily and lovingly practice self-care today."

Day 88

What you judge as negative in others, is usually a reflection of what you need to heal in yourself. Learn from them and then let go of your judgments. They only keep you small.

Three things for which I am grateful...

1.
2.
3.

Judging others is a learned behavior that focuses on other people and their perceived flaws. Maybe you know people like that. They have intense energy focused on what they see as negative things in other people that they believe shouldn't be there. But if a person is flawed (welcome to the human race) then those imperfections are there to teach that person what they need to learn. Judging them for it, is ultimately there to teach you to become more self-accepting and loving of others. If you are loathing them, look at what and how you internally loathe yourself. If you think they need to be perfect, look at your own perfectionism. Judging others is like a little road sign saying, "You still have some work to do. Keep your eyes on you."

One of the reasons I encourage you to work on this so much is that it permeates our society. Like a spreading cancer, from the cradle to the grave, we are taught that it's never enough. We are never enough. Being peaceful, loving and connected is not what the marketing tells us we need to be for happiness. No, you need to nip, tuck, scrape, buy, and acquire in order to be enough. Blessedly, I believe this is beginning to change as people become more aware and consciously choose to ignore the invitation to fix, fix, fix. If you live in and spread the value of be, be, be, you will find the happiness you seek.

What are the judgments you most make of others?

Do you see where the mirror is? It can be from your past or present behavior.

Are you feeling excited about seeing this so that you can transform it?

What are the possible implications for your life?

_____

_____

_____

_____

_____

_____

Take a moment and imagine what it feels like to live in non-judgement and non-attachment. List those feelings.

_____

_____

_____

_____

_____

_____

_____

_____

_____

_____

Affirmation:
"I gratefully learn from the mirrors in my life."

Day 89

Blow up your limiting beliefs. They were inherited and no longer serve. What you believe affects who and how you are in your life. Learn to truly look at them and prove them wrong. Unless, of course, they support your greatness!

Three things for which I am grateful...

1. _____
2. _____
3. _____

As you are now aware, beliefs are handed down generation to generation. They are woven into society, politics, tribes and families. Stop accepting what is not your inherent truth as truth. You have a right to challenge those beliefs. The ones that make you feel wrong, inauthentic, small, or powerless are lies. Guaranteed.

Faulty beliefs from my generation:

The American Dream which implies you are only successful if you work hard, have a family, two cars and buy a house. I must be thin to be happy. Men are more important than women. Uncle Sam will take care of us. Bleach and implants will make you happy. A pill will fix it. Young people don't know what they are talking about. A woman's place is in the home. The environment will fix itself. Why bother?

Faulty beliefs from the younger generations:

The number of likes means I'm worthy or not. Big lips and a big butt will make me happy. I must be thin to be happy. Social media makes me feel good about myself. The world owes me.

Anxiety is normal. Psychedelics will fix it. Old people don't know what they are talking about. The environment is screwed. Why bother?

Don't get locked in. It's not about making any one generation right or wrong, it's about letting go of limiting beliefs that keep all of us from living fully and harmoniously. Learn from everyone. Make your own decisions. Decide on your own truth but know that everyone is entitled to their truth as well.

What belief or beliefs have you had that keeps you from fully living your purpose and dreams?

Are you "willing to be willing" to let them go?

They no longer serve the new version of you. Your energy and vibration are moving beyond the "not enoughs" and into the YES, I deserve it all!

*A*ffirmation:
"I deserve what serves my Highest Good."

Day 90

You are deeply worthy
of all the love and beauty
in the world.

Three things for which I am grateful...

1.
2.
3.

On this journey, you have been challenged to do some very
powerful work. You have been presented with some ideas that
may be familiar or brand new to you. Or perhaps simply phrased
in a way that they can be heard differently. But if you have done
the work and made it to the end, you have been on a profound
journey of expansion. It is time to marinate on and integrate what
you have so courageously learned through our time together. I
have found that this work is the gift that keeps on giving. You will
continue to have lightbulb moments down the road.

Your Gratitude and Grace will forever carry you to new heights.
Congratulations and thank you for your heart.

**In celebration of your hard work and your vulnerability, we will
end our time together with a very powerful mantra. Before you
begin, write down your biggest takeaways from this work.**

Now, get comfortable. Give yourself a hug. Light a candle if
you'd like.

There is an ancient Sanskrit mantra you will now say 108 times.
It is said that to recite a mantra 108 times will help you align in
harmony with the very vibrations of the Universe.
The mantra is "Ananda Hum" and means "I am bliss" and
"My true nature is happiness."

Affirmation:
"Ananda Hum"

Congratulations!

You have completed your journey for this book!

Take a moment to really breathe in the energy of peace and completion for this courageous journey. Notice how far you have come and where you have transformed in your life. Remember how you felt when you started and feel into where you are now.

I acknowledge and applaud you for your courage to really look at yourself and take action for a better and more integrated you. May this journey bring you the gifts that you seek.

Remember that you came here to love. All of life is about creation, love and expansion.

Source Itself is love in motion, as are you.

You are in fact, a Magical Being of the Universe.

If you are interested in coaching one on one with me, go to WAKEUPwithJoni.com or email me at wakeupwithjoni@gmail.com .

Also check out my podcast, WAKE UP! With Joni on Apple Itunes or Spotify!

https://podcasts.apple.com/us/podcast/wake-up-with-joni/id1441920718?i=1000602992864

Acknowledgements

Alexandra: If we are lucky, we all have a muse. This book is inspired and dedicated to my beautiful daughter, @alliemichellel. As a child, I couldn't get her to read a book, so our mother-daughter connection, or "currency," became our nightly bedtime reading sessions. I would read to her until she became a voracious reader on her own. We would share and discuss different books and characters, marveling. I am forever grateful to Allie for fearlessly pursuing her own dream and sending her voice into the world through her poetry and fantasy books. I share her relentless belief that one person's voice can make a difference.

Allyuh: My new family on the Warrior's Path. You inspire and uplift me and one another on this path of discovery and freedom through your courage and kindness. May your journey be full of joy as you uplift one another and all of life.

John: You have surprised me, inspired me, loved me and guided me. You have brought joy and empowerment into my life and your sense of humor and sharing of the deep, deep well of Toltec Wisdom has brought a freedom of which I could only have dreamt. You have changed my life and I am profoundly grateful. As we offer the Medicine Wheel here on Paradise Ranch Retreat, my heart has found infinite dimensions of love.

Lori: My Sister. You have simply always been a part of my life. Like a twin and I am grateful for your humor, your curiosity, your courage and your support in navigating a world that is full of gifts or tribulations. So thank you for being my travel buddy this lifetime. You are the cool Auntie for sure. And the best sister ever.

Fred: For your continued presence in my life, three decades of marriage and two beautiful children. You truly are a man of great integrity, love and kindness. You are also a gifted healer and can be very proud of how many people you have helped heal and the father you are. I am forever grateful for our leg of the journey.

Jack: My dear friend and mentor. Thank you for your relentless belief in me and the tens of thousands of people you have taught and guided through the decades. You have made a lasting and profound difference in the lives of countless people across the world and continue to do so simply by being you.

Dean: As a fellow traveler on this path of empowering others to discover and embody their leadership genius, we have had many adventures for which I am deeply grateful. Your humor, integrity, and kindness are super powers. In your words, "Together, we are better than alone."

Shannon: Forty-five years is a long time to be friends. I love and appreciate you. We have always had each other's backs. Through thick and thin, the ups and down, the wild times and everything in between. Thank you for your love, friendship, wicked sense of humor and unapologetic authenticity. You inspire us all.

Printed in the USA
CPSIA information can be obtained
at www.ICGtesting.com
CBHW080430230924
14725CB00049B/813